D1397452

CONTENTS

Introduction to the St. Paul Center Studies in Biblical Theology and Spirituality

Scott Hahn, General Editor

The St. Paul Center Studies in Biblical Theology and Spirituality are a series of books designed to help Christians in their study of the Word of God. Dr. Scott Hahn serves as general editor, and the St. Paul Center for Biblical Theology, founded by Dr. Hahn, cosponsors the series with Servant publications.

Each volume helps to fulfill the mission of the St. Paul Center, which is to promote life-transforming study of Scripture in the Catholic tradition. The Center serves clergy and laity, students and scholars, with a variety of research and study tools, from books and publications to multimedia programs and a fully stocked Web library. All efforts promote and integrated study of the Word of God: the Old Testament with the New; the Bible within the liturgy; Scripture illumined by the tradition and the Magisterium.

We believe that every generation of disciples should know Jesus in the breaking of the bread (see Lk 24:13-37) and exclaim, as his first-generation disciples did: "Did not our hearts burn within us while he talked to us on the road, while he opened to us the Scriptures?"

TRANSFORMED BY GRACE

Scripture, Sacraments and the Sonship of Christ

DOM WULSTAN MORK, O.S.B.

The St. Paul Center Studies in Biblical Thology and Spirituality
SCOTT HAHN, GENERAL EDITOR

SERVANT
BOOKS

PUBLISHED BY ST. ANTHONY MESSENGER PRESS
CINCINNATI, OHIO

To Our Lady of Guadaloupe
and
for my Mother

Imprimi Potest: Rt. Rev. Gerald Benxert, O.S.B.
                    Abbot

Nihil Obstat: John A. Schulien, S.T.D.
                    Censor librorum

Imprimatur: William E. Cousins
                    Archbishop of Milwaukee
                    January 27, 1965

Cover design by Alan Furst
Book design by Phillips Robinette, O.F.M.

ISBN 1-56955-400-5

First edition published by Bruce Publishing Company in 1965,
Library of Congress Catalog Card Number: 65-18574

Servant Books is an imprint of St. Anthony Messenger Press.

St. Anthony Messenger Press
28 W. Liberty Street
Cincinnati, OH 45202-6498
www.AmericanCatholic.org
Printed in the United States of America

04 05 06 07 10 9 8 7 6 5 4 3 2 1

FOREWORD

This is the will of God: your sanctification.
—1 Thessalonians 4:3

We must never allow God's saving words to become shopworn.

Father Wulstan Mork never did. He was a monk, and he was a teacher. As a Benedictine monk, he lived a daily round of prayerful contemplation of the Bible. He read Scripture, he listened to Scripture, he sang Scripture. As a teacher—a high-school teacher!—Fr. Wulstan was always looking for fresh, simple and clear ways to present the eternal truths of the faith.

In his faithfulness to both vocations, he found a third: that of biblical theologian. And in his fidelity to this calling, he managed to make the most profound truths accessible to all.

This book is his biblical theology of the sacraments. I first discovered the book when I was a Protestant minister, and I found it compelling, convincing—and convicting. It's not that Fr. Wulstan built up a wall of proof texts that I just couldn't scale. He did something better than that. He identified a single unifying theme at the heart of Scripture: divine sonship. Then he moved easily through the entire Bible to demonstrate that divine sonship is the deepest meaning of our salvation, and the sacraments are the ordinary means by which we become children of God.

All other notions of salvation and sanctification pale in comparison. We cheapen grace, for example, if we treat it as simply "divine favor" or a merely legal act of forgiveness that brings us back to point zero. We cheapen holiness if we reduce it to decency and good behavior.

The grace of salvation is so much more. It is adoption. Yet even here the human categories fail us, for human adoption is a loving bond, and it is a legal bond—but it is not a natural bond. Divine adoption, however, is truly natural. In the Incarnation, God has taken on our human nature in order to give us his divine nature. The sacraments are a direct consequence of his Incarnation, and they are the means by which we become holy: "partakers of the divine nature."

Fr. Wulstan shows how sonship is imparted in baptism...matures in confirmation...is nurtured in the Eucharist...and is restored in penance. He shows us how our own resurrection is prepared by anointing, and how by holy orders the priest enters into the fullest share of

Christ's own sonship. Likewise, marriage is not only for the procreation and education of offspring—that's natural marriage. The *sacrament* of marriage is for the procreation and education of *divine* offspring.

As a teacher, Fr. Wulstan liked to play a game with his students. He would add five extra points to their grade if they answered immediately his question, "What are you doing?" with "The will of God!" Whether they were reading, eating, studying, playing—whatever—he wanted them, first of all, to be doing the will of God.

And the will of God worked itself out according to a single, unified plan. Fr. Wulstan saw it prepared in the earliest pages of the Old Testament, when man and woman were created in the image and likeness of God. He would have loved the words of the *Catechism*: "Thanks to the unity of God's plan, not only the text of Scripture but also the realities and events about which it speaks can be signs" (n. 117).

The Fathers of the church called this unity the "divine economy"—God's fatherly plan for creation and redemption. This is not just a book about how God utilizes matter in the sacraments or about how God imparts grace. It is, rather, about the divine purpose from the beginning.

These ideas were not platitudes for Fr. Wulstan. Nor can we afford to treat them that way ourselves.

In his sixty-ninth year, our good monk suffered a stroke. The necrology of Marmion Abbey tells the rest of the story: "Due to complications from the stroke and diabetes, he lost one leg, and then the other. In keeping with his teaching over many years, he accepted these sufferings as 'the will of God.'"

For the author, the teachings of this book were hard won and, eventually, subject to the most rigorous trial.

Such was the will of God: the sanctification, the divine sonship of Wulstan Mork. The good monk gloried in that will.

He teaches us to do the same.

Scott Hahn
General Editor

INTRODUCTION

Many Catholics would like a manual of the spiritual life, a guide to Christian living, that would be complete as to doctrine and also provide a practical program. We have such a "manual" in the three liturgical books, the missal, the ritual, and the pontifical, for these contain the forms and accompanying prayers of the sacraments. The Christian life is sacramental, and we can say that the spiritual life of the individual Catholic is supernatural activity which derives from the sacraments as its source and framework. Baptism and confirmation are continuing acts, and the faithful Catholic lives by them every day. Baptism and confirmation form an atmosphere for him as well as a powerhouse.

  I have written this book as a commentary on the sacramental acts, seeking mainly in the Bible for the mind of Christ as to what he intended his sacraments to be. When we realize that the Son became man to give us the Holy Spirit who would join us to himself in baptism, thus making us truly adopted children of God the Father, we come to appreciate that in all the sacraments we are led by the Spirit to be sons of God (cf. Rom 8:14). Their purpose is to form us into Christ. We greatly need to see our Catholic life as a unity, to simplify. And it is a unity— Christ. The sacraments are acts that make it possible for us to act daily toward the Father as adopted sons in the Son.

This is the chief theme of the book, and I present it especially to the laity with the hope that in these very bewildering times it will help them to grasp the depth and the simplicity of the Church's life. For many Catholics today the pressing concern is to achieve a synthesis between the supernatural and the natural. We read and hear, for example, such expressions as "changing times," "Christianity must be meaningful for today's world," "and involvement in the world"—all indeed are true. But such a synthesis already exists in the life of the sacraments, which are themselves supernaturalized human signs and acts, given here and now to this individual, and whose graces are tailored particularly to him in his situation. We must look to the sacraments, therefore, for this synthesis.

My greatest debt of gratitude is to my abbot, the Rt. Rev. Gerald Benkert, O.S.B., for his blessing, encouragement, and permission, also for his directing me to the biblical notion of man's spirit. I owe much gratitude to the members of my abbey for many things, especially to Father Joseph Battaglia, O.S.B. and Father Leo Grommes, O.S.B., who provided time to write. I want to thank the editorial staff of the Bruce Publishing Company, particularly Mr. William E. May, who has been a most understanding and congenial editor; Fr. Vladimir Vancik, for his generous loan of books; the boarding cadets of Marmion Military Academy, who have patiently listened to much of the book; and Mrs. Carl Berkhout, who so kindly and capably prepared the manuscript for the publisher.

Marmion Abbey,
Aurora, Illinois,
January 10, 1965

ONE

Split-Level Living

Most Catholics feel they live on two levels. We can call it split-level living. On one they live their religion; on the other, the rest of their life. They give time and effort to religious duties, but when these have been taken care of, they descend, as it were, to daily life as to a lower plane. They fail to relate religion to living.

These persons will begin the day with morning prayers, at least a morning offering. Then they get down to "life": breakfast, work, coffee breaks, lunch, more work, dinner, TV, social and civic duties. Before bed there is a short jump up to the higher level for night prayers. Of course, some jump up to that level at other times during the day by saying the rosary, making occasional ejaculatory prayers or a visit to the Blessed Sacrament. Some may even go to daily Mass and Communion and do a bit of spiritual reading. But there is always the consciousness that one is living on two levels, that here is religion, and, on the other band, here is life. One lives two lives, and they never seem to get together. As a result, a person tends to acquire two attitudes: The one toward his religion, that it's necessary, and, at least in theory, the most important thing in his life; the other toward the rest of life, that it's necessary too, but somehow unrelated to his religion. At times he even has the guilty feeling that some of it is opposed to his religion. And he feels guilty, too, because be finds "life" more downright enjoyable than religion.

Does this sound like schizophrenia? Not really, although the schizophrenic lives on two levels, too. But just as a split personality is not good, neither is split-level living; in fact, it's completely wrong. The reason: there can be no such thing. There cannot be two levels in our life because for us Catholics there is only one that we can possibly live on, and this is the supernatural.

Come, you say, what about eating, and working, and playing golf, all perfectly good acts, willed by God. These are natural, arising from the needs of the natural man. We can't give up the necessities of life. Why, even the Trappists eat, sleep, and work.

Read again the first sentence of the chapter. People *feel* that they are living on two levels. Their purely religious acts they would call supernatural, and those pertaining to "life," natural. Many "supernatural-ize" the latter by means of the morning offering, the good intention, but that very fact gives evidence to their attitude. They regard the areas of their life that center around its human necessities as being purely natural.

This, however, is an entirely false position. There is no such creature as the isolated natural man, not even in the remotest Australian bush. All men are on the supernatural level, at least as to the purpose of their life—the beatific vision.

To understand this fact, which can and should change our life, we must turn to God's own revelation in the Bible, in particular to the account of his creation of man in the Book of Genesis. "God said, 'Let us make mankind in our image and likeness....'" "God created man in his image. In the image of God he created him."[1]

How is man the image of God? God's revelation to man was a gradual thing, progressive, adapted to his condition; Christ gave the *fullness* of revelation. Hence the New Testament enables us to understand and interpret the Old, just as the main part of a speech explains the general points that the speaker indicates in his introductory part. St. Paul has told us in what this "image of God" consisted: "...put on the new self, created after the image of God in the justice and holiness that come from truth," and "Strip off the old self with its deeds and put on the new, which is being progressively remolded after the image of its Creator and brought to deep knowledge."[2] The image of God, in which man was originally created, is sanctifying grace. A great Greek Father, St. Gregory Nazianzen (died about 390), wrote of Christ's restoration of sanctifying grace as "...a restoration of the image which had fallen through sin."[3]

We can best understand what man originally was by what he lost, by what Christ restored. For St. Paul fallen man was "the old self," deprived of sanctifying grace; "the new self" was the new man in Christ, to whom Christ by his death and resurrection gave back "justice and holiness," and "deep knowledge," Pauline expressions for sanctifying grace.[4] What else is this grace but the elevation of man to God's life, to a plane of living supernatural to man, so that he can know and love God as God knows and loves himself?

Thus man, created in God's image, was originally a reflection of God's very life, because in some way, by God's favor, he shared in it. As a fact, man lost this life because of original sin, but God's intention was from eternity to restore it to him through the Messiah—Christ. Even after the fall, man was, therefore, on the supernatural level, at least as to his final end.

Later books of the Old Testament, too, unfold the meaning of earlier ones. A passage in the Book of Wisdom is more explicit about the meaning of "image of God." "For God formed man to be imperishable; the image of his own nature he made him."[5] In context these words mean that as man shares in God's life so he will share in God's happiness.[6] But God's happiness consists in knowing and loving himself. Therefore man was created for this supernatural purpose.

St. Gregory of Nyssa (died about 395), another of the great Greek Fathers of the Church and friend of St. Gregory Nazianzen, considered the "image of God" to be sanctifying grace. He wrote: "...man was created to the image of God; which is the equivalent of saying that God made human nature a sharer in all that is good." But this seems equivalent to saying that God gave man all that he is, all his goodness. "Wherein, then, lies the distinction between the Divine and that which resembles it? In this: that the one is uncreated and the other exists through creation."[7] "In Gregory's theology, man 'was made like God in all things.' As God's image he possesses in his finite way every excellence that is to be found in God. Implicitly, therefore, man is holy, somewhat as God is holy."[8]

The whole Old Testament is emphatic on this one point: God is not merely a force, an energy, but a *person*. (There is no revelation of the existence of three persons in God until Christ's coming.) He has not only being, but also intellect and will. In making man in his image, that is, a creature capable of the closest possible union with him, he made man a person too, for the only basis for union with God by a creature is on the personal basis: person to person.

Adam shared God's life and was intended by him for the beatific vision after he passed his trial—and that trial consisted of Adam's freely choosing God as his good by means of his own intellect and will—the act of a person. To be a person was then the necessary basis for the beatific vision.

The Bible nowhere says that man's *soul* was created in God's image, but *man*—the whole man, since he is a composite of body and soul. It is true, God has no body, but since man's soul is whole and entire in every part of his body, the latter is to feel the effects of sharing in God's life now, and later, of the beatific vision.

Since man was created in God's image, which is sanctifying grace, then man without sanctifying grace is a freak. A harsh word, yes, but it best expresses the reality; something that should have been in man is missing. It's like being born without a leg. This gap in man we call original sin. We did not sin in the Garden of Paradise, our protoparent did; and because even at that time we and all human nature were in him, we "lost out," we were deprived of that according to which and for which we were created—God's life. And because of this "something missing," our whole being, at least unconsciously, cries out for it. We are an orientation demanding fulfillment; we can only be fulfilled by God in the beatific vision *because he made us that way*.

This is a universal condition, this applies to all. St. Gregory of Nyssa wrote, "...the whole of human nature from the first man to the last is but one image of him who is."[9] The true image, grace, was lost, but each man is a potentiality for this image and a capacity, just as a coffee cup is by its creation a capacity for coffee. It may be used as an ornament or a planter, but its end is frustrated unless it contains that for which it was made.

But, you may object, sanctifying grace is a pure gift from God, man doesn't have it coming to him. In other words, a man can be a man without it. Yes and no. True, grace is pure gratuity on God's part and we *could,* at least in theory, be perfect human beings without it. But in the concrete, man was *created* in grace, destined for fulfillment in the beatific vision, and so he cannot be a man, as God intends him to be, without it. To repeat,

God could have created man on the merely natural level and *then* given him grace. But he did not. Grace was a part of man—although a supernatural part—from his very creation. That is the reason why we had to begin with the fact that mankind was *created* in God's image, in order to understand that there is no such thing for man as the isolated natural level.

This is a good place then to discuss the meaning of the words "natural" and "supernatural." Nature makes a thing what it is, its very essence. There are animal, vegetable and mineral natures, with specific natures in each of these. There is spiritual nature, with man a blend of this and animal nature. A thing acts as it does because of this essence. Thus, a vegetable grows, a cricket chirps, a stone rolls, a man works a math problem. Whatever we can say of a thing depends on its nature: water is wet, people are funny (and sometimes weird), sulphur smells foul. Comic-strip animals are not natural because their actions proceed from human, not animal, nature.

What about "supernatural"? In general the word refers to something that is over and above nature. But the Christian use of the word means something that properly belongs to God and which he freely gives to man. Or, we can say that supernature is God's gift of himself to man. Anything that is supernatural to man, then, must be:

1. something that belongs to God as God,
2. which a man does not need to be a man, and
3. which is entirely above his merits.

Man does not *need* the beatific vision to fulfill him as a human, nor does he *deserve* it. And nothing he can do can merit it. This is a free gift of love from God.

But God did give Adam this tremendous gift and its "seed," sanctifying grace, and he gave it not *after* he created him nor *as* he created him, but *because* he created him. Man came into being solely for the beatific vision, his happiness was to be a "by-product." Even when Adam lost this gift, God intended to give it back through Christ. Hence I can say that the Australian bushman is on the supernatural level, at least as far as his destiny is concerned, and that for us Catholics, baptized in Christ, there is only one level on which we can live, the supernaturalized natural.

Every man who was ever born and who will be born has therefore an *almost* natural desire for the beatific vision.[10] And since he does, there must be in every man some supernatural—shall I say, potential?—for it.[11] What this is will be the subject of the next chapter; for now to know that it exists is sufficient.

We can better understand this if we take a good look at the Catholic doctrine of hell. The Church's teaching is that every person—including our bushman—who dies in mortal sin will go to hell. Dying in mortal sin means knowingly and deliberately rejecting God even at the end of one's life. The bushman may never have heard of the God of the Christians, but he must during life have faced the fact that a Supreme Being exists, that he has definite obligations, and that there has to be a reward or a punishment. Now what is the worst suffering in hell?

We think of it as physical, but it's not: it is the realization of the loss of God in the beatific vision.

But the beatific vision is entirely supernatural to man. Therefore there must be in every man such an orientation to the beatific vision that his worst punishment can be its eternal loss.[12]

There is a passage in St. Luke's Gospel which has often been interpreted as demanding a heroic degree of renunciation: "He who is bent on saving his life must part with it anyway; but he who freely parts with his life for my sake will save it in the end."[13] The word for *life* in the Greek original is *psyche,* which is often used in the New Testament for the life of the soul on the natural level. The meaning of the passage, then, becomes this: He who rejects the supernatural to live wholly on the natural level is going to frustrate his supernaturalized nature; if he lets supernature take its course, he will fulfill the end for which God created him. A similar verse in St. John's Gospel substantiates this interpretation: "He who holds his life *(psyche)* dear destroys it; he who sets no store by *his life in this world* will preserve it for *eternal life.*"[14]

There must be no split-level living. If, as St. Augustine puts it, "...nothing but Absolute Being can satisfy human nature,"[15] it is not only wrong but also false to make the people and things in our life ends in themselves. We end up in what we call the "rat race" reaching for a pill or a drink or groping for the analyst's couch. We cannot live on the purely natural level because there is no such thing. It is a never-never land, which is the reason why the effort to live in a "purely natural way" proves to be so unsatisfactory. If we frustrate our basic orientation to God we frustrate ourselves not simply as Christians, but, more radically, as human beings.

The movement in Western civilization known as the Renaissance was the attempt to free man from the supernatural, and the literature, art, and history of the West ever since have suffered accordingly. You can no more divorce the natural in man from the supernatural than you can his animal element from his rational. In fact, the definition of man as a rational animal is incomplete in the light of the Bible. Rather, man is a spiritual animal.

Every man has a basic tendency toward the beatific vision, a desire for truth and good, which can only be satisfied by this supernatural end. Hence, there is in each one of us a "something" that reaches up constantly for God and for fulfillment by God. We call this "spirit."

Notes

1. Gen 1:26-27. (Unless otherwise specified, Old Testament quotations are taken from the Confraternity of Christian Doctrine edition.)

2. Eph 4:24; Col 3:10. (New Testament quotations are from the Kleist-Lilly translation, published by The Bruce Publishing Company, Milwaukee, 1956.) For this interpretation of these two texts cf. Fernand Prat, S.J., *The Theology of St. Paul* (Westminster, Md.: The Newman Press, 1961), Vol. II, p. 73. Man is basically God's image in that he has intellect and will—by which, like God, he can know and love. Sanctifying grace given to man, then, means that he participates more

fully in God's nature and life, and thus he is to some degree an image of that nature and life. Cf. Sister M. Charles Borromeo Muckenhirn, C.S.C., *The Image of God in Creation* (Englewood Cliffs, N.J.: Prentice-Hall, Inc., 1963), p. 53.

3.   *Orat.*, 40, 7. In Philip Schaff and Henry Wace, eds., *Nicene and Post-Nicene Fathers* (New York: The Christian Literature Company, 1894), Vol. 7, p. 361.

4.   We shall not find the term "sanctifying grace" in the Bible. Instead the reality of God's life in us is revealed by such expressions as "justification," "holiness," "the kingdom of God," "the charity of God," "the adoption of sons." When St. Paul speaks of "grace" his emphasis is rather on its gratuitousness. We must try to understand the Bible according to the meaning of the sacred authors, not our terminology.

5.   Wis 2:23.

6.   Cf. Paul Heinisch, *Theology of the Old Testament* (Collegeville, Minn.: The Liturgical Press, 1950), p. 170.

7.   *De Hominis Opificio,* 16. *P.G.* 44, 184. Quoted in Henri de Lubac, S.J., *Catholicism* (New York: Longmans, Green and Co., 1950), p. 209.

8.   Walter J. Burghardt, S.J., *The Image of God in Man According to Cyril of Alexandria* (Woodstock, Md.: Woodstock College Press, 1957), p. 82.

9.   In de Lubac, *op. cit.,* p. 5.

10.   Cf. Richard Bruch, *Theology Digest*, 1960, p. 25 ff.

11.   Cf. J.P. Kenny, S.J., "Reflections on Human Nature and the Supernatural," *Theological Studies,* 1953, p. 286.

12.   If this seems a little rough on non-Christians let's not approach the matter with our emotions but with our intellects. If the non-Christian would only turn off his radio long enough to face the basic realities, he could come up with the answers I gave with regard to the bushman. If, then, he does, sincerely worships and obeys this God—who in reality is the true God, only by another name, perhaps—and is sorry for having offended him, and is ignorant of the Church through no fault of his own, he has baptism of desire. God is love.

13.   Lk 9:24.

14.   Jn 12:25. Cf. Gal 6:7-8.

15.   *The City of God,* Vernon Bourke, ed. (New York: Image Books, 1958), p. 392.

T W O

The Spirit of Man

We know that man is on the supernatural level from God's own word in the Bible. Since we could never come to that conclusion from reason or science, neither of these can tell us what man *really* is. Even when both have concluded that man must be soul and body they have not told us all. To know the complete man we must turn to God's revealing word.

It is noteworthy that the Bible never *divides* man into body and soul. It recognizes that man is composed of these two diverse elements, but always takes man as a unity, a composite. The body as the "prison of the soul" is not biblical language, but that of Greek, specifically Platonic, philosophy.

The usual biblical words to express man considered as man are *flesh* and *soul;* the Bible's view of man as a composite is reflected in the fact that it often says *flesh* or *soul* when it really means the whole man, body and soul.[1] Here are two examples of their interchange-able use: "[God] said to Noah: The end of all flesh is come before me, the earth is filled with iniquity through them, and I will destroy them with the earth." "Who is the man that feareth the Lord? …His soul shall dwell in good things."[2]

Flesh and *soul* in the Bible mean man as a human being, taken in his solidarity with the rest of humanity and God's earthly creation. They can also mean man turned inward upon himself, as living for self-ish motives. We could say that these two words seem to denote that man is on the natural level but there is a third word pertaining to man in the Bible—*spirit*. This is revelation's contribution to understanding the composi-tion of man.[3]

We read in Job: "But it is a spirit in man, the breath of the Almighty, that gives him understanding." And these words of God to Moses: "Take Josue, the son of Nun, a man of spirit, and lay your hand upon him." Another example, incorporated into the Offertory prayers, is this passage from Daniel: "…nevertheless in a contrite heart and humble spirit let us be accepted."[4]

These are only a very few of the many references in the Bible to man's spirit. From a careful study of them all in their context we see that the spirit is not a man's soul, nor a part of him, but rather a dimension, one that directs him vertically to God. In contrast with spirit, a man's "flesh"—the natural combination of body and soul—is horizontal, earth-and-self-directed.

When we say that someone is spirited we mean that he's lively; again, when we say that they sang with spirit, we mean they sang with life. Life is basic to the idea of spirit. Then there is that elusive thing, school spirit; how many times convocations and editorials have tried to define it! The common agreement here is that it is equivalent to love of one's school, a going out of oneself to be interested in the school as well as in its activities. The popular notion of "spirit," then, is that it is something quite alive, outgoing, directed to others, to charity, and to the true, good, and beautiful. It is something in a person that drives him to unselfishness and self-forgetfulness, and, in a natural way, to wonder and contemplation.

In the Old Testament, from the time of Isaiah on, if a man was faithful to God's will, he acted by reason of his spirit. If his conduct was dictated only by natural motives, then the mainspring was his "flesh." "Spiritual" behavior was regarded as something divine-human, a cooperation of a man's spirit with God's Spirit, which in the Old Testament meant God's creative power.[5] Hence, spirit meant man's orientation to God, his leaving the horizontal plane of self and natural-level living to achieve by God's help some measure of union with him.

St. Paul most clearly presented the meaning of spirit. Fr. Charles Davis, the popular English theologian, wrote of him and of this presentation: "He is thoroughly Hebrew in outlook; he saw a man simply as a unity. Consequently his antithesis of flesh *(sarx)* and spirit *(pneuma)* is not an opposition between matter and spirit, between body and soul. 'Flesh' is not a part of man; but the whole man in his weakness and mortality, in his distance from God, and in his solidarity with a sinful and corrupt creation. 'Spirit' is man as open to the divine life and as belonging to the sphere of the divine, man under the influence and activity of the Holy Spirit. Flesh and spirit emerge as two active principles affecting man and struggling within him."[6]

We see this clearly in the passage from the Epistle to the Galatians, 5:16-24. It begins with these familiar words: "Walk in the Spirit, and you will not fulfill the lusts of the flesh. For the flesh lusts against the spirit, and the spirit against the flesh; for these are opposed to each other, so that you do not do what you would." St. Paul is opposing, not body to soul, but the biblical meaning of flesh, that is, natural man, to spirit, his supernatural tendency. The whole selection must be read with this particular meaning in mind. I would refer you to St. Augustine in his *City of God* (Book 14, Chapters 2–5), who explains the passage at length.[7]

The French Catholic philosopher Claude Tresmontant has summed up the distinction between flesh and spirit nicely: "The spirit is man's participation in the supernatural order. The spirit summons him to the destiny of a god.... Hence the spirit-flesh opposition does not mark a duality within nature itself as does the dichotomy of body and soul. It is in fact a distinction between the order of nature and the supernatural which is a revealed order."[8]

We can define spirit, then, as man's capability for supernatural union with God, the "processing," especially of his intellect and will, for contact with God on the level of sanctifying grace, and, ultimately, of the beatific vision. It is because of his spirit that a person is oriented to God, that he seeks the true, good, and beautiful, which, in their infinite existence are God, that he goes out of himself toward love, which is another name for God.[9] I would compare spirit to the vulcanizing of rubber, say, of a piece of rubber to be used for the bit of a pipe. The natural substance is not really fitted for this function, so it has to be processed for the purpose. Or spirit is like a beautiful, naturally talented voice. It is fundamentally a voice just like anyone else's, only this one is capable of singing the most beautiful and difficult songs and arias. You see, spirit is not an *addition* to the human person, but that person "processed" for the purpose of a spirit-to-Spirit relationship.

A person's spirit is not due to him as a man, it is strictly supernatural, and is explained only by his radical orientation to the beatific vision. The Protestant biblical scholar Eduard Schweizer says that St. Paul regards it as "...God's gift and so ultimately alien to man.... Paul never says that the soul finds its completion in spirit. Where he does actually mention the idea of an 'organ' which receives the Spirit of God, he also calls it 'spirit' and expressly describes it as something not belonging to man but given to him by God (Rom 8:15-16; 1 Cor 2:11)."[10]

Everyone is on the supernatural level, at least as to his end, therefore everyone has spirit. In every man there is this capability, this "talent" for union with God, to be fulfilled by grace and beatific glory.

> The Holy Spirit does not create the "spirit" in man; it is potentially present in every man, even if rudimentary and undeveloped. Every human being has affinities with the spiritual and the eternal. In each individual of the race *the spirit of the man which is in him* [1 Cor 2:11] answers to the Spirit of God, in so far as the finite can correspond with the infinite; though there are men who are psychic [*psyche* = man living on the natural level] and not spiritual, who may even be said not to "have spirit" [Jude 19], human nature is incomplete without it, and vainly seeks satisfaction in sensual or even in intellectual enjoyment [Eph 4:17 ff.].[11]

A man's spirit is his point of contact with the Holy Spirit. H.B. Swete wrote of this: "...the human spirit lies dormant and powerless till it has been awakened and enabled by the Spirit of God."[12] St. Paul is emphatic on this point: "For those who live on the natural level are concerned merely with what pertains to human nature, but they who live by the spirit, with what pertains to the Spirit." "He who sows in his flesh, will, out of that flesh, reap corruption; but he who sows in the spirit, will, by the Spirit, reap eternal life."[13] Fr. Reypens, S.J., commenting on Chapter 14, verses 14-16, of the First Epistle to the Corinthians, says that here and elsewhere in St.

Paul's epistles spirit designates "...the spirit of man insofar as he is under the action of the Holy Spirit, and as such is distinguished from the simple intellect...."[14] And the great authority on St. Paul, Fr. Prat, S.J.: "Now the latter [spiritual man] indicates a relation to the Spirit of God, source of the supernatural...."[15]

To understand better the relationship of a man's spirit with God we must turn again to the account of man's creation in Genesis: "Then the LORD God formed man out of the dust of the ground and breathed into his nostrils the breath of life, and man became a living being."[16] The Hebrew word for "breath" in this passage is *neshamah,* which is interchangeable with *ruah.* Both words mean "spirit," but their basic meaning is, first, "breath," and, second, "a wind."

The Genesis text in itself means only that man has life, something he has in common with animals, nothing more.[17] Yet in Chapter 3 of the same book God says: "My spirit [breath] shall not remain in man forever, since he is flesh,"[18] as if to imply that the breath of life in man is in reality the breath of God, something in man and yet not quite belonging to him. The same idea occurs in the Book of Job: "So long as I still have life in me and the breath of God is in my nostrils.... For the spirit of God has made me, the breath of the Almighty keeps me alive.... If he were to take back his spirit to himself, withdraw to himself his breath, all flesh would perish together, and man would return to the dust." Another passage in Job, already quoted, credits more to this breath of God than mere life: "But it is a spirit in man, the breath of the Almighty, that gives him understanding."[19]

And by the time of Isaiah, as has already been noted, this breath is understood as being an orientation to God in man: "The Egyptians are men, not God, their horses are flesh, not spirit . . . ."[20] Breath is a most apt as well as beautiful figure for man's capability for union with God: it designates not only life, but also a bond between God and man, something of God in man, that keeps him turned to the source of his breath. Dust he has in common with all creation; breath, in common with God.[21]

I shall continue this idea in Chapter 3, after we have considered the Person of the Holy Spirit. In summary of these first two chapters we can conclude: (1) that man has been created on the supernatural level and (2) that therefore there is in him, in each one of us, a tendency toward the beatific vision, an orientation of the whole person for this supernatural end—spirit. Before we learn more of this end and the means to it we must understand as much as we can of him who is our End in that vision, God, who is three Persons.

Notes

1. The Hebrew word for "flesh" is *bashar,* and for "soul," *nephesh.* The Greek for "flesh" is *sarx,* and for "soul," *psyche.*
2. Gn 6:12; Ps 24:12-13 (Douay-Rheims version).
3. The Hebrew word for "spirit" is *ruah,* also *neshamah,* and the Greek is *pneuma.*
4. Job 32:18; Num 27:18; Dan 3:39.

5.   Cf. Walter Eichrodt, *Theology of the Old Testament* (Philadelphia: The Westminster Press, 1961), Vol. 1, pp. 388-389.

6.   Charles Davis, "The Resurrection of the Body," *Theology Digest,* 1960, p. 100.

7.   *The City of God,* Bourke, ed. (New York: Image Books, 1958), pp. 295-303.

8.   Claude Tresmontant, *A Study of Hebrew Thought* (New York: Desclée Company, 1960), p. 109. Cf. Jn 6:23. Also cf. Joseph Fichtner, O.S.C., *Theological Anthropology* (Notre Dame: University of Notre Dame Press, 1963), pp. 4-18.

9.   1 Jn 4:8.

10.   Eduard Schweizer and others, "Spirit of God," in Gerhard Kittel's *Bible Key Words* (New York: Harper and Brothers, Publishers, 1961), Vol. III, pp. 85, 86.

11.   Henry Barclay Swete, *The Holy Spirit in the New Testament* (London: Macmillan and Co., Ltd., 1910), p. 342. Cf. J.P. Kenny, S.J., "Reflections on Human Nature and the Supernatural," *Theological Studies,* 1953, p. 286.

12.   Swete, *op. cit.*, p. 395.

13.   Rom 8:5; Gal 6:8. The translation is mine from the Greek.

14.   L. Reypens, S.J., "Âme," *Dictionnaire de Spiritualité,* Vol. I, column 435.

15.   Fernand Prat, S.J., *The Theology Of St. Paul* (Westminster, Md: The Newman Press, 1961), Vol. II, p. 404.

16.   Gen 2:7.

17.   Cf. Bruce Vawter, C.M., *A Path Through Genesis* (New York: Sheed and Ward, 1956), p. 53.

18.   Gen 6:3.

19.   Job 27:3; 33:4; 34:14-15; 32:8.

20.   Is 31:3.

21.   Cf. Dominique Barthélemy, O.P., "Le Souffle du Dieu Vivant," *La Vie Spirituelle,* April, 1963.

THREE

The Act of God

We now realize that by our very creation as human beings we are intended for the closest union with God that is possible for creatures, and that each one of us is a living capacity for this union. God is our end, and has to be, therefore, our life. But, you say, what is God? Who is he? I must know the answer to these questions if I am to be motivated to God-orient my life.

We, whose culture and background have been European, have made the mistake of thinking that we can analyze God, "figure him out," get him down on a slide under a microscope. We have put him on the level of people and things that we can know. We must face this very humbling fact: We cannot *know* God. Some years ago a popular song called him "the man upstairs," an expression that reflects the popular notion that God is a superhuman, and thus is completely knowable.

St. Gregory of Nyssa has put us presumptuous mortals in our place very well:

> Men have never discovered a faculty to comprehend the incomprehensible; nor have we ever been able to devise an intellectual technique for grasping the inconceivable. For this reason the great Apostle St. Paul calls God's ways unsearchable (Rom 11:33), teaching us by this that the way that leads to the knowledge of the divine nature is inaccessible to our reason.... Such then is He Whose essence is above every nature, invisible, incomprehensible.[1]

There exists, then, this infinite distance between God and us, *and yet we shall know God.* This is just what we have been discussing in the first two chapters—the fact that God *created* us for this knowledge of him, the beatific vision, and that we tend "naturally" toward this knowledge. If God had created us on the natural level, of course we could not know him. Our destiny, to know God, is superhuman, supernatural. In Chapter 6 we shall take a closer look at the beatific vision, but here, by realizing its supernatural character, we realize our natural inability to know God. Yet God has told us certain things *about* himself, and we call this deposit of knowledge "revelation." This is, by its very name, God gradually revealing himself. The full unfolding of this revelation was the work of Christ, and Christ committed this revelation, this work, to his Church, whose essential mission is the proclamation of the good news revealed in Christ to mankind.

Revelation tells us what God is. But our intellect, without this knowledge, can grope toward some understanding of him. This latter is the way of philosophy; the first, that of faith. The various notions of philosophers regarding God indicate the fallibility of the intellect in this pursuit, and yet there is a sort of common-denominator conclusion about God that those who honestly think about the subject agree on.

Therefore, if we dare to define what and who God is we must turn to revelation. When God spoke to Moses from the burning bush, giving him the mission to lead the Israelites out of Egypt, Moses asked him for his name. "God replied, 'I am who I am.' Then he added, 'This is what you shall tell the Israelites: I AM sent me to you.'"[2] The Hebrew word in the text for "I AM" is *Yahweh,* God's name in the Old Testament. Theology has accordingly defined God as *being from himself,* which definition is in contrast with that of *creature:* being from another. God is the source of his being, which then is eternal and necessary. The creature, produced by another, begins and can cease to be. Only God necessarily *is*.

But Christ revealed that God is one in three Persons, a Trinity. This is a strict mystery that the intellect alone could never discover, nor even now can it understand. Remember the catechism definition, "one God in three divine Persons"? I find this definition a little misleading, because when most people say the word *God* they at least unconsciously think of only one Person. Rather, as a workable definition, I would propose this:

the Trinity is three Persons possessing simultaneously the one divine nature.

Before we can consider the divine nature we must clearly understand the meaning of *nature*. In Chapter 1 we discussed this in relation to *supernature,* but it is so very important that we are agreed on just what a nature is that I am going, more or less, to repeat the matter. A nature is that which makes a thing what it is; it is its essence, what it is. We are human beings because we have human nature. When we read of some brutal crime, we say, "How inhuman!" Somebody let his human nature get unbalanced. Action follows nature, proceeds from it. Dogs bark, flies are pesty, little children tend to dart from between parked cars, all because of their particular natures. It is their nature that makes bricks hard, leaves green, and liederkranz pungent.

The divine nature is that which makes God *God,* and we have already seen that this consists precisely in being from *himself.*[3] This being must be eternal and necessary. People who are sheepish about saying *God* and who are culturally several cuts above those who call him "the man upstairs," may refer to him as the Supreme Being, and they are quite right in their designation. The very notion of God is of *the* supreme being, for if there were one who was supreme to God, he would be God. Our intellect concludes that this being-from-himself-supreme-being also has to be all-perfect, or, as theology would say, infinitely perfect. Infinite means *without limits,* and so, if there were one limit to one of God's perfections, we would have to look elsewhere. God must possess all good, he must be all good—all truth, good, and beauty.

Therefore there can be no parts in God. What is a part but incompletion? It *needs* other parts for some function or to make up a whole. A part is imperfect in itself. But God is perfect, it is his *nature* to be perfect. We can thus argue that he cannot be a material substance, for matter is always composed of parts, even a simple element. God's essence or nature has to be nonmaterial, or spiritual.

We know, to our constant chagrin, that our perfections, if we have any, are quite detachable from us. We may have worked on patience for a long time, and there comes a day when we feel we're entitled to say, "Now I am patient." And then before nightfall something happens and we lose every shred of our hard-won virtue. And the humiliating thing about all this is that with or without patience our own human nature remains intact. The good in us is indeed detachable and temporary. Yet in God's nature this cannot be. His perfection has to be not only eternal but also one with him, because detachableness is itself an imperfection. So we cannot say that God is just or merciful but rather we say that he *is* his justice and mercy. In other words, God is *simple,* simple in the sense of one essence, with no parts, no accidental additions, no change.

From revelation and reason we know that God has intellect and will, or rather, in view of his simplicity, that he is his intellect and will. These, of course, are infinitely perfect, and therefore are eternally occupied in knowing and willing himself. The intellect, whether in God, angel, or man, pursues truth, and the will, good. But God is infinite truth and good, so if I may reword the Roman playwright Terence the proper occupation of God is God.

All of this is a bit glib, and we must constantly realize the infinite gap that exists between the divine nature and human nature. All that revelation has told us of God, all that reason can discover, are no more than the back of God after he has passed by. That is all Moses was allowed to see, and for us in the way of faith his face is not now to be seen.[4] Like the Israelites and their golden calf or the Jews at the time of Christ who wanted *their* notion of a Messiah, we want God to be on our level, thoroughly understood, and, yes, manageable. We hear occasionally of someone who quits the Church because he's "mad" at God for taking a loved one in death. Rather silly gesture when we consider who and what God is and who and what we are.

The divine nature is possessed simultaneously by three divine Persons. This is the truth about God. Christ revealed the existence of persons in God, also their names: Father, Son—who he is, and Spirit. Before we can proceed we must grasp the distinction between person and nature. A person is an agent of action, his nature is the basis for his action, out of which and by means of which he acts. John is a person and he acts as a human being because he has human nature, but he alone is responsible for his conduct because he alone is the agent of that conduct. Person, then, is the *who,* nature is the *as what*. Since person implies responsibility for action, only a being endowed with intellect and will can be a person. The normal dog is hardly a person, although Mr. Charles Schulz's supreme comic creation Snoopy is a person because Mr. Schulz invested him with intellect and will.

In the Trinity there are three agents of action but only one nature. It is completely repugnant to say that there are three natures in the Trinity because of the idea of the divine nature—it has to be one because it has to be supreme, the highest. Three equally divine natures could not be. There are not co-Gods. The three Persons have the one, same nature, therefore they have the one, same intellect and will. They are equally God, equally infinitely perfect, equally eternal. Although the divine nature is simple, the Persons are really distinct from each other. We are in the presence of a strict revealed mystery, and now, as never before, do we realize that we cannot analyze God. We gratefully receive this revelation from God and believe his word.

Basing themselves on the revealed names of the divine Persons the early Greek and Latin Fathers of the Church attempted some understanding of the mystery.[5] Father and Son imply the act of generation. But since God is spiritual, not material, the human and animal mode of generation is unthinkable. What is God's essential activity? It is knowing and willing himself. Now a thought can be said, metaphorically, to be generated by the thinker. Don't we call the products of our thinking "brain children," and isn't an idea also termed a concept?

Hence the Son proceeds from the Father by intellectual generation, as his thought. And what is this thought? God's intellect is occupied in knowing himself, and, since God is simple, this thought is the one complete expression of all that God is. That is, the Father gives the Son all that he is, except his being Father, and he does this by conceiving all that he is as a thought. If this seems too human an explanation, it indeed is. In the matter of the Trinity we have to proceed by way of metaphor, "in a glass, darkly."

It will help us here if we realize just what a thought, or idea, is. When our mind conceives an idea of some object it makes a composite of the essential elements of that object. For example, the idea of a book, what precisely makes it a book and not an apple, would consist of the fact that it is a number of pages that are in some way held together. This idea of "bookness" expresses perfectly the reality of every book in creation. So the idea of God, the Son, generated by the divine intellect in the Father, expresses perfectly the reality of God.

By the act of human generation a man is able to reproduce himself, and, although there are the genes and chromosomes of the mother to contend with, it often happens that a son is truly a "chip off the old block," the image of his father. God the Son is the exact image of his Father, because all that the Father is, he is—all except the fact that only the Father is Father; the Persons are distinct from each other as persons.

God's essential activity consists in knowing and willing himself. The Son is God's knowledge of himself, the Holy Spirit is God's love of himself. We must realize that loving is willing: when we love another what we are really doing is (1) willing, or wanting, him as our good, and (2) willing his good, his welfare.[6] Love, then is basically an act of the will, and the Holy Spirit proceeds from the divine will as the love of Father and Son for each other.

On Easter evening when Christ appeared to the Apostles in the upper room "...he breathed on them and said: 'Receive the Holy Spirit....'"[7] He had already revealed the name of the third Person of the Trinity; by this action of breathing he demonstrated how the Holy Spirit proceeds from the Father and himself—as breath.

We know from Chapter 2 that the root meaning of *spirit* is breath. Now breath is not only a sign of life but an important element of it. Another thing to note is that a breath, when it is an exhalation, goes out of a person, and, I might add, when someone is in love, his breath is so often a sigh of love that not only goes out of him but also is directed to the one loved. Hence the Holy Spirit is the sigh of love of Father and Son for each other, he is the very personification of their love. St. Thomas Aquinas wrote of the procession of the Spirit from Father and Son: "So what proceeds in God by way of love, does not proceed as begotten, or as son, but proceeds rather as spirit; which name expresses a certain vital movement and impulse, accordingly as anyone is described as moved or impelled by love to perform an action."[8]

Let us see how this relates to what was said in the past chapter about spirit. In the Old Testament the breath, or spirit, of God is used metaphorically to express God's power in creation, his dynamism. The New Testament tells us that the spirit of God is really a Person. Linking these two facts we can say that the Holy Spirit is God's power. But he is the love of Father and Son for each other, which love is itself power—as is all love—a creative force in the Father directed to the Son, and in the Son directed to the Father.

God's breathing into man the breath of life was, first, a manifestation of his power; second, a power-act proceeding from his love, which love was directed to himself in man, his image and likeness; third, a giving to man that which in God is God-directed, breath, so that by means of this breath, or spirit, man might himself be God-oriented.

Part of the mystery, we know, is that although the Son proceeds from the Father and the Holy Spirit proceeds from both, there is perfect equality of Persons, and there is no question of time. In fact these processions did not take place once in the past, and ever since we have the three Persons. They are taking place now, for God lives in the eternal now. We have to revise our notion of eternity. It is not something stretching infinitely backward and forward, but a boundless now.

It would be good at this point to read rapidly the Gospel of St. John, looking for references to the three divine Persons. Not to substitute for this but to help, I shall cite some of the texts, grouping these under main headings.

Christ, the incarnate Son, is equal to the Father, implying that each possesses the one divine nature: "'My Father,' he said, 'has been working to this hour; and so I, too, am working.' The result was that the Jews were all the more eager to kill him, not only because he broke the Sabbath, but also because he spoke of God as his own Father, thereby claiming equality with God." "All men are to honor the Son just as they honor the Father. He who does not honor the Son does not honor the Father, whose ambassador he is." "If you knew me, you would also know my Father." "The Father and I are one."[9]

Because of their having the same divine nature Father and Son are inseparable: "...you will understand that the Father is in me and that I am in the Father." "Do you not believe that I am in the Father and the Father is in me? Take the words I speak to you: they are not my invention, are they? And as for the things I do, the Father who dwells in me, is personally responsible for them. Believe me, all of you, when I say that I am in the Father and the Father is in me; but if not, at least believe on the strength of what I am doing."[10]

The Father gives his being to the Son: "Whatever the Father possesses is mine...." "I want them to behold my glory, the glory you bestowed on me because you loved me before the world was founded."[11]

As to his divinity, Christ proclaims that he is the Son: "'Do you believe in the Son of God?' ... 'You are now looking in his face,' replied Jesus; 'Yes, it is he who is now speaking to you!'" "Father, the hour is come! Glorify your Son, that your Son may glorify you."[12]

The Son is only-begotten: "...and we have looked upon his glory—such a glory as befits the Father's only-begotten Son—full of grace and truth!" "He who believes in him [the Son] is not liable to condemnation, whereas he who refuses to believe is already condemned, simply because he has refused to believe in the name of the only-begotten Son of God."[13]

That the Holy Spirit proceeds from Father and Son can be inferred from these texts: "And I will ask the Father, and he will grant you another Advocate to be with you for all time to come, the Spirit of Truth! ...the Advocate, the Holy Spirit, whom the Father will send in my name...." "...for he who is God's ambassador [Christ] proclaims God's message; besides he communicates the Spirit in no stinted measure." "Unless I depart, the Advocate will not come to you; whereas, if I depart, I will send him to you."[14]

Because of their relationships with each other, the Persons of God have certain roles in the Trinity. The Father is the Source: "Just as the Father is the source of life, so, too, has he given the Son the power to be a source of life...." "...I live because of the Father...."[15] The Son is the glory of the Father, which he gives by being the Father's image, and by his love. In the human father-son relationship, the son gives his father glory by consciously imitating him, thereby acknowledging that his father is worthy of imitation. Love is the highest form of glory, for love is choosing, willing someone as good, and to love one above all others is to admit that that person is the superlative of goodness. The Holy Spirit, the love of Father and Son, is their union, for love unites.

These Trinitarian roles are the same in the relationships of the divine Persons outside the Trinity, with us. The Father is for us Source and End. Our religion must be the Father-centered religion of the Son. Just read the prayer of Christ to the Father after the Last Supper (Jn 17) for a most moving example of this. Look through the missal to see that the Mass and most of its prayers are directed to the Father. Christianity is *to the Father through the Son in the union of the Spirit.* Through Christ, in him, with him, we give the Father the twofold glory of being in Christ's image and of love; and uniting us to Christ and forming us into his image is the role of the Spirit in our regard.

God is not a static being, God is act, and that act is the procession of Persons in the Trinity, now. This is God's life, and because he has created us to partake in this life, precisely as adopted in the Son, the act of God is not merely an example to us, which, if we have a "devotion" to the Trinity, we should imitate, but a downright, essential necessity, *by which* we live. The result is Trinitarian work, sleep, eating, even Trinitarian golf, and, perhaps, a Trinitarian martini. This is so because of God's redemptive act.

Notes

1.   Cited in Jean Daniélou, S.J., *From Glory to Glory* (New York: Charles Scribner's Sons, 1961), pp. 98-99.

2.   Ex 3:14.

3.   Good supplementary reading would be Walter Farrell's
         Companion to the Summa (New York: Sheed and Ward,
         1941), Vol. I, pp. 56-65.

4.   Cf. Ex 33:18-23.

5.   Cf. Matthias Joseph Scheeben, *The Mysteries of Christianity*
         (St. Louis: B. Herder Book Co., 1946), pp. 73-117.

6.   Cf. Wulstan Mork, O.S.B., *A Synthesis of the Spiritual Life*
         (Milwaukee: The Bruce Publishing Co., 1962), pp. 87-94.

7.   Jn 20:22.

8.   *Summa Theologiae,* Part I, question 27, article 4. Translation
         by the English Dominicans (New York: Benziger Brothers,
         Inc., 1947).

9.   Jn 5:17-18, 23; 8:19; 10:30.

10.   Jn 10:38; 14:10-11.

11.   Jn 16:15; 17:24.

12.   Jn 9:35-37; 17:1.

13.   Jn 1:14; 3:18.

14.   Jn 14:16, 26; 3:34; 16:7.

15.   Jn 5:26; 6:57.

F O U R

The Redemptive Act: Atonement

God created man in his image, which was sanctifying grace. Although Adam possessed this likeness of God's nature, his relation with God was still that of a creature to his creator. It was a general relationship to the three divine Persons. The grace that Adam lost for the human race was restored to it by the Son—through and in the Son, and thus some theologians see as the great difference between Adam and us the fact that we are adopted sons whereas he was not![1] The new creation, which is the Christian life, is union not only with the divine nature but also with the divine Person of the Son, so that we might be by adoption what he is by nature.

The purpose of Christ's redemption was to confer adopted sonship on the human race. "But to as many as welcomed him he gave the power to become children of God—those who believe in his name...." "He [the Father] predestined us to be adopted through Jesus Christ as his sons...."[2]

The basis of our relationship with the Son is the human nature we have in common with him ever since he became man. If we regard human nature as being one, as we did in Chapters 1 and 3, and as that which is essential to man as man, then this fundamental relationship with Christ becomes not only clear, but also astounding: by the fact that he and we are human beings we are brothers! Our one human nature makes us brothers with all men, but in this case it makes us brothers with God the Son. "The Word became flesh," says St. John, and the biblical meaning of *flesh* is body and soul together, i.e., human nature.

> The basic fact is that the Incarnation established between the enfleshed Word and human beings a twin relationship: exchange and solidarity.... He took what is ours, to give us what is His. Second, the condition of this exchange is the solidarity of all humanity with Christ.... The origin of the solidarity is the human nature of Christ.[3]

If all men are brothers of Christ, all are sons of the Father in a basic sense. Just what, then, is the purpose of the Church? Is not this general fatherhood of God and brotherhood of man enough? They would be if the purpose of the Incarnation were merely for the Word to become flesh. But its purpose was directed to a further end—the redemptive act, the giving of the Spirit, who would then make us adopted sons in a very real sense.

As true men, Christ and we have flesh in common. But are we flesh alone? Are we not also spirit—that orientation to union with God that is in each one of us? And is Christ flesh alone? Is he not also—and principally—God, having within himself the Father and the Spirit? And is not the Spirit in Christ the fulfillment of his orientation to union with the Father, because he is that union? So union with the flesh of Christ is not enough. God wills to give us, in Christ, the Spirit, who will unite us to Christ, and, in and through him, to the Father. The purpose of the redemptive act is the union of our spirit with the Holy Spirit, and by him the union of our totality with the totality of the Son, with his divine and human natures.[4]

Our basic sonship in Christ has to be fulfilled by his conferring on us adopted sonship. The general brotherhood of man is a good thing, but this bond is slight in contrast with that between natural or adopted brothers. Why stop with being sons-in-general to God the Father when he offers us the privilege of being adopted sons?

St. Cyril of Alexandria says that adopted sonship is given us in two sacraments: baptism and Eucharist. In baptism we participate in the Holy Spirit, and in the Eucharist, in Christ's human nature.[5]

Is not the purpose of baptism the remission of sin—original and actual—plus the giving of sanctifying grace? What's all this about participating in the Holy Spirit? Furthermore, why the emphasis on the Holy Spirit in relation to the redemption? Did not Christ suffer and die to atone for sin, merit grace, and win back heaven for us?

We can only go on what Christ has revealed. Hence, putting aside all other points of emphasis, which developed in order to combat heresies and dangerous tendencies in the history of the Church, let us turn again to the Bible. In speaking of Christ, St. John the Baptist said: "He for his part will baptize you in the Holy Spirit— and in fire." And Christ, in the Gospel of St. Luke: "Now, then, if you, bad as you are, are disposed to give your children useful gifts, how much more readily will the Father in heaven give the Holy Spirit to those that ask him!" The parallel passage in St. Matthew (7:11) has "what is good" in place of "the Holy Spirit," an indication that Christ's intention is to give all the good things that he has merited when the Father and he give the Holy Spirit.

But in the Gospel of St. John the relation of the Spirit to the redemption is more marked: "I am telling you the plain truth: unless a man is born of water and the Spirit, he cannot enter the kingdom of God! What is born of the flesh is flesh, and what is born of the Spirit is spirit." "On the last and solemn day of the feast, Jesus stood erect and cried out: 'If anyone thirsts, let him come to me and drink. He who believes in me will, as the Scripture has said, himself become a fountain out of which streams of living water are flowing forth.' He meant by this the Spirit whom those who believed in him were destined to receive. As yet there was no outpouring of the Spirit, because Jesus was not yet glorified."[6]

To sum up the argument from these few passages: in baptism the Father and Christ give us the

Spirit, who gives us sanctifying grace with its resultant beatific vision, the infused virtues, the seven gifts, and actual grace, all of the good things merited by Christ's redemption. The Spirit, like a fountain, is, then, a source, the source of supernatural life in us.[7]

I shall discuss St. Cyril's teaching on our sonship as realized in the sacraments of baptism and Eucharist later, in the chapters devoted to these sacraments. But I believe that now we are able to formulate the thesis of this book. As a diagram it would look like this:

Spirit

↓

Father → Son → Spirit → Son → Father

The Father sends the Son, made flesh by the Spirit (hence "Spirit" is placed above "Son"); after the Ascension, the supreme glorification of the Son, he and the Father send the Spirit, who creates the Church. But what is the Church but the Mystical Body of the Son, forming, as it were, one Person with him? The Son is now the "whole Christ,"[8] head and members, which is the reason for the second "Son" in the diagram. The work of the Holy Spirit is not to form Christians but the whole Christ. Christians are adopted sons in the Son; the Spirit, who is union in the Trinity, unites the whole Christ to the Father. The process by which Christ and the Holy Spirit are giving adopted sonship in its various degrees of depths, completing Christ in each one and in the Mystical Body, is the work of the sacraments.

> But when the designated period of time had
> elapsed, God sent his Son, born of a woman,
> born in subjection to the Law, in order to
> redeem those who were in subjection to the
> Law, that we might receive the adoption. And
> because you are sons, God sent the Spirit of
> his Son into your hearts, crying, "Abba.
> Father." You are, then, no longer a slave but a
> son; and if a son, an heir also through God's
> grace.[9]

Everything is in this passage from the Epistle to the
Galatians. But let us examine more closely the role of the
Son in the redemptive act. He was "born of a woman,
born in subjection," but why? "In order to redeem." We
must note this well: the purpose of the Incarnation is the
Redemption. Catholic spirituality, beginning in the
Middle Ages, has tended at times to "get lost" in one or
another of the more appealing aspects of Christ's humanity.
As a result, many have never been able to "see the woods
for the trees." They have not seen Christ whole. And this
is one of the things that validly irks Protestants. We give
them the impression of following a Christ of special devotions rather than the Christ of revelation.

Father Durrwell writes: "The Incarnation is still
the central mystery, but to be effective, it must reach its
full flowering in glory by way of Christ's death."[10] "So
marked, indeed, has been God's love for the world that he
gave his only-begotten Son: everyone who believes in him
is not to perish, but to have eternal life."[11]

The doctrine of the hypostatic union means that
Christ is one divine Person—that of the Son—and two

natures: the divine, which he has in common with his Father and Spirit, and the human, a true, created human nature, body and soul. Therefore the human nature is not in itself a person. Recall, person means *agent of action,* the one who acts out of his nature. If there were two persons in Christ there would have to be two agents of action, and we would not be redeemed; for everything he did as man would have been done by a man only and would hardly have had infinite value. But, nevertheless, he is also truly human—another mystery, which now cannot be fully understood. And Christ's human nature, being without its own person and completely taken over by the Person of the Son, is therefore God.

It is true, the Son took a human nature so that as God-man he could atone for man as man. Revelation is emphatic on this point. For example: "By sending his Son in the likeness of sinful flesh as a sin-offering, he has condemned sin in the flesh, in order that the justification of the Law might be fulfilled in us, who walk not according to the flesh but according to the spirit." "For our sakes, God made sin of him who knew no sin, so that in him we might become God's holiness."[12]

But notice in each of these passages the purpose clause, and hence the purpose of Christ's atonement: atonement for sin was not the end of the redemptive act, it was a condition. Its end is to give us the power to live "according to the spirit, so that in him we might become God's holiness"—sanctifying grace, given by the Spirit to our spirit in the Son. Atonement is a necessary condition for this new mode of living, for we cannot be adopted sons and yet have this unpaid debt of reparation to be made to God, nor can we have anything in us of sin. Christ's atonement took care of reparation and sin; and it not only entirely annihilated all past sin but also made it possible for us to have the victory over sin in the future. And so sin is not to be a preoccupation for the Christian, but sonship; not death, but life. The redemptive act is not terminated by Christ's death, but by his Ascension.

Just as the Incarnation was necessary for atonement for sin, so also was it necessary for the ultimate purpose of the atonement, the adoption of sons. Human beings are to be adopted not only by the human nature of the Son but also by their solidarity with that nature. It is adoption through and in the incarnate Son.[13] The prayer the priest says at the Offertory when he mixes a little water with the wine expresses this: "Grant us through the mystery of this water and wine to be sharers in the divine nature of him who chose to share our human nature...." Exchange and solidarity, for atonement and sonship. When we realize that we are adopted in the very real humanity of the Son, we come to realize that our adoption is something very real.

What is the relation between Christ's atonement for sin and his meriting of grace? He accomplished both by his death, but is there any connection? Recall that Adam lost the image of God, grace, for himself and all men by his sin. By this act he turned from God to himself, choosing self as his good instead of God. This was a free and willing choice. How could he share in God's life after that? Add to the first, or "original" sin, the almost infinite number of human choices of self, the turning away from God, down the years to ourselves included, and the relation between grace and sin is apparent. The life of God cannot exist, let alone thrive, in a person who has willingly rejected God. If God is to restore the divine life to man, man must turn again to God by choosing him as good instead of self. Man did this, the whole human race did this, turned back to God, in Christ. How? By the human will in Christ choosing God as its good, and choosing it even unto death. "He humbled himself and became obedient to death; yes, to death on a cross."[14]

The atonement had to consist, first, in Christ's heroic, constant, and perfect obedience—obedience that was perfect love, and therefore choice of God. "Now obedience is preferred to all sacrifices…. Therefore it was fitting that the sacrifice of Christ's Passion and death should proceed from obedience."[15]

"For our sakes God made sin of him who knew no sin…." As the "last Adam…imparting life" he took on himself all sin, past, present, and future, as if he were the very personification of sinful man, and from the beginning of his earthly life until his death united his human will with the Father's, for us and as us. "'Here I am; I have come to do your will, O God.' …It is in virtue of this 'will' that we have been sanctified through the offering once for all of the body of Jesus Christ."[16]

Christ's constant choice of the Father, which was, in practice, choosing the Father's will, led to his sacrificial death. His obedience was the basic prerequisite;

the actual atonement was, by the Father's will, to be accomplished by his passion and death. His whole earthly life was one source of meriting, but the great act of choice, the essence of the atonement, was his death. His earthly life was ordered to it, prepared for it.

He offered himself to the Father as a willing victim, out of love for the Father and for man. "The Father loves me because I lay down my life.... I lay it down of my own will. I have power to lay it down, and power to take it back again. Such is the charge I have received from my Father." "...the world must come to know that I love the Father and am acting strictly according to the Father's instructions. Rise; we must be going on our way." "...I live by faith in the Son of God, who loved me and sacrificed himself for me."[17]

The essential element of a sacrifice is not the death of a victim but the fact of offering. St. Augustine wrote in *The City of God:*

> There is, then, a true sacrifice in every work which unites us in a holy communion with God, that is, in every work that is aimed at that final Good in which alone we can be truly blessed.... Our body, too, is a sacrifice when, for God's sake, we chasten it, as we ought, by temperance.[18]

Our morning offering makes everything in our day a sacrifice because we offer it to God out of adoration and love. Thus everything in our day *is made sacred,* which is the literal meaning of the word *sacrifice*. The death of Christ was not a sacrifice because it was a death but because he offered himself to the Father for that death, and made it sacred by offering it to the Father as the personification of the human race, and, therefore, for the human race.

The two greatest punishments for original sin were the loss of the divine life and its consequent beatific vision, and death. The first was supernatural, the second, natural. Death was the greatest natural punishment because man is composed of soul and body; both have to be united if a man is to be a human being. Human nature no more resides in the soul alone than it does solely in the body. So the worst possible natural thing that can happen to a man is the destruction of his human nature.[19] The sacrificial death of Christ not only restored to man the divine life, but also destroyed death, giving back the immortality of the body. We shall see this better in the next chapter, but let us realize now that the incarnate Son had to submit to death himself in order to do away with death. He died for us, in more ways than one.

Notes

1. Cf. Walter J. Burghardt, S.J., *The Image of God in Man According to Cyril of Alexandria* (Woodstock, Md.: Woodstock College Press, 1955), p. 118.
2. Jn 1:12; Eph 1:5. (The latter is the Confraternity translation.)
3. Burghardt, *op. cit.,* p. 107.
4. Cf. Rom 8:14-17.
5. Burghardt, *op. cit.,* p. 113.
6. Mt 3:11; Lk 11:13; Jn 3:5-6; 7:37-40.
7. Cf. William Barclay, *The Promise of the Spirit* (Philadelphia: The Westminster Press, 1960), pp. 21-45.

8.   St. Augustine, *In Psalm.* 56. Cf. Erich Przywara, S.J., *An Augustine Synthesis* (New York: Harper Torchbooks, 1958), pp. 217, 218.

9.   Gal 4:4-7.

10.   F.X. Durrwell, C.S.S.R., *The Resurrection* (New York: Sheed and Ward, 1960), p. 40.

11.   Jn 3:16.

12.   Rom 8:3-4. (The translation is that of the Confraternity edition, which here translates *sarx* and *pneuma* literally as "flesh" and "spirit." The whole of Chapter 8 should be read at this time.) Cf. 2 Cor 5:21.

13.   Cf. Lucien Cerfaux, *Christ in the Theology of St. Paul* (New York: Herder and Herder, 1962), pp. 161-172. Canon Cerfaux corrects a possible false impression one could get from St. Cyril's emphasis on our general sonship in Christ.

14.   Phil 2:8.

15.   *Summa Theologiae,* III, Q. 47, a. 2.

16.   2 Cor 5:21; 1 Cor 15:45; Heb 10:7, 10.

17.   Jn 10:17-18; 14:31; Gal 2:20.

18.   St. Augustine, *The City of God,* Bourke ed., pp. 192-193. Cf. *Summa Theologiae,* III, Q. 48, a. 3.

19.   The seat of the human personality is the soul, but separated from the body it is unfulfilled, because human life is an interaction of soul and body.

FIVE

The Redemptive Act: Resurrection

The essential act by which Christ atoned for sin and merited adopted sonship for man was his death and the sufferings that led up to it. We know this; it is one of the fundamentals of our religion. But another fundamental, which we may not know, is that by his death Christ merited for himself. How else do we explain his words to the two disciples on the way to Emmaus on Easter itself: "Was it not necessary that the Messiah should undergo these sufferings and thus enter into his glory?"[1] Christ merited his own resurrection as well as his glorified body.

Further—and more important—Christ merited first for himself, and only then for the human race. It was necessary that this be so. "Yet our Lord had become so completely one with the race of Adam that what he wished to gain for us he first gained for himself," writes Fr. Durrwell.[2] Yes, he had to first gain for himself, because, being the new Adam, what he would give to others he must first have in himself. "Son though he was, he learned obedience through what he suffered, and after he had been raised to the heights of perfection, he became to all who obey him the cause of eternal salvation, since God had proclaimed him a high priest after the manner of Melchizedek." "And of his fullness we have all received a share—yes, grace succeeding grace...."[3]

St. Paul wrote to the Philippians:

> Be of the same mind as Christ Jesus, who though he is by nature God, did not consider his equality with God a condition to be clung to, but emptied himself by taking the nature of a slave, fashioned as he was to the likeness of men and recognized by outward appearance as man. He humbled himself and became obedient to death; yes, to death on a cross. This is why God has exalted him and given him the name above all names....[4]

Christ's resurrection was the reward for his "emptying himself" of the prerogatives of his divine nature, taking an ordinary human nature, and choosing his Father's will, even "to death," by his human will, for himself and for man. And thus he merited for himself in the reunion of his soul and body the restoration of Adam's original privilege, deathlessness: "...since we know that Christ, having risen from the dead, will die no more; death shall no longer have dominion over him."[5]

The passage from Philippians reminds us of the fact that before the resurrection Christ's human nature was to all appearances as human as everybody else's. His contemporaries could conclude that although he obviously was a man of God, he was just as obviously a man. He slept, soundly, in fact, as he did in a boat during a storm; he got tired and had to rest; he was hungry and thirsty; and his way of getting around was hardly supernatural: he walked, like everyone else. Miracles and signs and great wisdom, but all proceeding from a man, with a hometown and relatives and a trade. He could weep at the death of a friend, whom a few minutes later he would resurrect. And especially his sufferings and death proved that he was a man. All could see him suffer, grow faint, bleed, and die.

The question arises: Was this right? Should the human nature so closely united to God that it does not even have its own person be such an ordinary human nature? Could it not have been a real one, with a true body and soul, and yet freed from all human weaknesses such as hunger, fatigue, and suffering, and, above all, from the punishment of death? It should have been completely glorified, as it was after the resurrection, the kind of a human nature God the Son ought to have. It should have been, but it could not have if the Son became man in order to redeem. The redemption meant obedience, suffering, death.

And so because Christ "emptied himself," appearing on earth not as God-man but as man, and especially because he "humbled himself" to the extreme degree of accepting the common human punishment of death, he merited for his human nature the glory that it ought to have had and did not have before his death.

St. Paul wrote to Timothy: "He was made visible in his human nature, vindicated in his spiritual nature...."[6] "The Resurrection," writes Durrwell, "revealed the true condition of this man which had up till then been hidden beneath the servile aspect of a carnal humanity."[7] The Son had to be vindicated, his identity had to be made known. (Somewhat as the true identity of the prince who has been incognito as a valet for two acts is finally revealed in the third.) Especially since Christ by dying was associated with sin, death being a punishment for the original sin, it had to be shown that, contrary to all previous appearances, he was absolutely and in every way sinless.

With the resurrection Christ's humanity appears to be that of God the Son. If he eats, it is only to prove the reality of his risen body. He can pass through closed doors, he is no longer subject to the natural physical laws. What has happened is that the divine Person of the Son has at last exercised his rights over his human nature: it has become the *kind* of a human nature that the Son *ought* to have. To parallel the expression of St. Paul quoted above, from the resurrection on Christ is "recognized by outward appearance" as God; and he is recognized because he is recognizable. Yes, at the resurrection Christ was "...patently marked out as the Son of God by the power of that Spirit of holiness which raised Him to life again from the dead."[8]

Let us contemplate the risen Christ—radiating glory, holiness, and life, because now his human nature is able to radiate his divinity. Now his body is completely under the control of his Sonship.

"'The first Adam became a soul having life'; the last Adam became a spirit imparting life."[9] Christ is not only the new Adam, but infinitely superior to him; as the Son-made-flesh he can be called the firstborn in relation to creation, giving a life superior to that given by Adam. The new head of the human race is God, and a God-man, one in solidarity with the race. As all of human nature was in Adam, so is the principle of supernatural life in Christ, as the potential of his new race.

> Further, he is the head of his body, the Church, in that he is the beginning, the first to rise from the dead, so that he may have preeminence over every creature. For it pleased God the Father that in him all fullness should dwell, and that through him God should reconcile to himself every being, and make peace both on earth and in heaven through the blood shed on the cross.[10]

Only at the resurrection does Christ become a *perfect* image of the Father.[11] Only then, therefore, is he perfectly Son. Of course, his human nature was united hypostatically to the Son from the first instant of the Incarnation, and was, because of that union, truly God. But, as I said previously, it was not the nature that ought to be so united to the Son because it was subject to human weakness and the imperfection of change. The Son is the image of the Father, who is perfection. Not until his human nature can be in every way perfect can the Son image the Father in that nature. So we can say that only by the resurrection does the human nature of the Son experience the full effects of the hypostatic union, of the divine Sonship.

Therefore only the *risen* Christ can give adopted sonship. The Son merited adoption for us by means of his human nature. Should we benefit from that merit before the very instrument of meriting? Should we receive sonship before Christ's humanity is in every way Son? Sonship is given by our organic union with Christ, not only with his divine nature, but also with his human, with him as a totality. Christ must attain to the fulfillment of his own Sonship before he can be the source of adoption.

I have quoted St. Paul as attributing the resurrection to the Holy Spirit (Rom 1:4). Before we can see the relation of the Holy Spirit to the conferral of adopted sonship we must first see his relation to the incarnate Son.

Christ was conceived by the Spirit: "The Holy Spirit will come upon you, and the power of the Most High will overshadow you." After Christ's baptism by John "...the Holy Spirit descended upon him in bodily shape like a dove...." Then, "Jesus, full of the Holy Spirit, turned away from the Jordan and was led by the Spirit into the desert to be put to the test by the devil for forty days.... Invested with the power of the Spirit, Jesus now returned to Galilee...."[12]

The Holy Spirit is the love of Father and Son, therefore he is their union. Each gives himself to the other by means of the Spirit, for love is the giving of self. The Spirit gives the self of the Son to the human nature, in the womb of Mary, uniting that nature to the Person of the Son. His role with regard to Christ from that instant is still his Trinitarian role of union—influencing the human nature by love which is his own Person, uniting Christ's human will with the will of the Father. Because of love of his Father, Christ goes to the desert to fulfill his will; for the same reason he leaves it for Galilee.

The Spirit also personifies holiness in the New Testament; he is the only Person who is qualified by the word *holy*. What is holiness but the very essence, the nature of God? The words of the *Gloria* "you alone are holy" mean that "you alone are God." Holiness, then, is synonymous with God. "Holy, holy, holy" is the most simplified expression of a person completely seized with the realization of God. Now the holiness of God is not static but dynamic, it is act. The Spirit is this dynamic holiness insofar as it is love—God giving and being given.

In the Old Testament the *Spirit of God* means

> ... a creative, transforming power, and its purpose is to create a sphere of religion and morals.... It is active power, that is to say, it is the personal activity of God's will, achieving a moral and religious object.[13]

Revelation is an unfolding process. What is revealed as God's power in creation in the Old Testament is shown by Christ to be personification of that power. Thus St. Luke can write that the Incarnation was the work of "the power of the Most High," and that Christ was "invested with the power of the Spirit." The human nature of Christ was created; hence the immediate divine action on that creation was the work of the Spirit.

If the body of Christ is to be reunited with his soul, this also is to be the work of the Spirit as God's power in creation. "True, though he was crucified through weakness, yet he lives through the power of God." The resurrection is attributed to the Spirit, because it is an act not only of power, but also of union and holiness. At the instant of reunion the Holy Spirit enables the human nature to experience the full influence of Sonship, that is, of the holiness that is in the Son. Now "...the life that he lives is a life for God."[14] No more will the demands of the body for the body's sake have to be satisfied. Holiness prevails, because it is the "...Spirit of holiness which raised Him to life again."

The purpose of the redemption is to give adopted sonship. This has already been stated, but it must be repeated here because it summarizes the foregoing and is a premise on which we can continue. The risen, glorious Christ is now capable of conferring adoption. But the actual adopting is done by the Holy Spirit as agent for Father and Son.

> For all who are moved by the Spirit of God are sons of God. The Spirit you have received is not a spirit of slavery leading you back into a life of fear, but a Spirit that makes us sons, enabling us to cry "Abba! Father!" In that cry the Spirit of God joins with our spirit in

testifying that we are God's children; and if
children, then heirs.[15]

We are sons because of the action of the Spirit of
adoption.

There is a parallel between his action upon the
humanity of the Son and upon the humanity of the
adopted sons. As the power of God in creation, as union,
and as personified holiness, he gives the nature of
adopted sonship to our human nature in the instant of
baptism. From then on we are "moved by the Spirit of
God," impelled by him as power, able to cry "Father!"
to God the Father because we have dwelling within us
the Spirit of the Son.

The end of the redemption is sonship, it is true,
but there is a first and immediate end, the giving the
Spirit, who then gives sonship. Recall the diagram
expressing the theme of the book:

Spirit

↓

Father → Son → Spirit → Son → Father

The Son has redeemed, and, therefore, merited sonship
for man. But what the Son has merited the Spirit gives,
as God's immediate contact with man. Sent by Father
and Son, the Spirit is active in this his era, the "Time
after Pentecost." But the Son is active, too, as the source.
As Henry Barclay Swete nicely put it: "The
purpose of the Son's mission was to give the rights of

sonship; the purpose of the Spirit's mission, to give the power of using them."[16]

The Spirit is God's point of contact, but what is man's? "...the Spirit of God joins with our spirit...." Our point of contact with God is our spirit, that "breath of God" within us which orients our whole being to him, which makes every person in the world long for sonship—spirit to Spirit.[17]

Notes

1.   Lk 24:26.
2.   F.X. Durrwell, *The Resurrection* (New York: Sheed and Ward, Inc., 1962), p. 56.
3.   Heb 5:8-10; Jn 1:16. Cf. *Summa Theologiae,* III, Q. 7, a. 9; Q.8, a. 5.
4.   Phil 2:6-9.
5.   Rom 6:9.
6.   1 Tim 4:16.
7.   F.X. Durrwell, *op. cit.,* p. 47.
8.   Rom 1:4, in J.B. Phillips, *Letters to Young Churches* (New York: The Macmillan Company, 1958), p. 2.
9.   1 Cor 15:45.
10.   Col 1:18-20.
11.   Cf. Durrwell, *op.cit.,* p. 128.
12.   Lk 1:35; 3:22; 4:1-2, 14.
13.   Friedrich Baumgärtel, "Spirit of God," in Gerhard Kittel's *Bible Key Words,* Vol. III (New York: Harper and Brothers, Publishers, 1961), pp. 1-2.
14.   2 Cor 13:4; Rom 6:10. Cf. Col 2:12.
15.   Rom 8:14-17. The translation is that of *The New English Bible* (Oxford: University Press, 1962).
16.   Henry Barclay Swete, *The Holy Spirit in the New Testament* (London: Macmillan & Co., Ltd., 1910).
17.   Cf. Rom 8:19-23.

The Redemptive Act: Sonship

The parallel action of the Holy Spirit on Christ's humanity and on man has a parallel result: at the Incarnation he united the Son with a human nature; at baptism he unites the Son with a human nature. What is the difference? In the latter case he unites the Son, possessing not only the divine nature but also the human nature he received at the Incarnation, with a purely human person. The result is not the hypostatic union—two natures in one divine Person—but adoption.

Sonship is conferred on man through union with Christ, the Son by nature. This union is a very real, organic union, not something symbolic or metaphorical. Christ himself used the metaphor of a vine and branches to express the reality, St. Paul used that of head and body. But these figures of speech are revelation's way of conveying the overwhelming truth of this union.

> Further, he is the head of his body, the
> Church.... For it pleased God the Father that
> in him all fullness should dwell, and that
> through him God should reconcile to himself
> every being, and make peace both on earth
> and in heaven through the blood shed on the
> cross.[1]

The fullness of divine life that fills the glorified Christ
can be given only by an organic union with him.[2] The
union is *organic* because it is necessary for life. The
leaves of a plant must maintain an organic union with
the stem if they are to live; the knuckles need such a
union with each other and the palm of the hand. Flowers
in a vase are hardly organically united with each other,
for there is no mutual dependence for life.

The parts of the body are necessarily joined
together, and especially with the head, which is regarded
as the source of life for the rest of the body. From the
head come food, water, air, as well as direction. Sever the
body from the head, in other words, sever the organic
union, and death results. It is true, the head needs the
body also for its life; the metaphor, like all metaphors,
"limps," but what it tells us of our union with Christ is
that it is one similar to the union of head and body
because we depend on Christ for life. He, the risen
Christ, is the source. In him is "all fullness."

And so we form with him the nearest thing to a
person without being essentially God—the "whole
Christ," the Mystical Body. That is the reason why
adopted sonship is ours *as a result* of this union with

Christ: because of the "whole Christ" we participate in his most fundamental condition, his Sonship. Christ has a number of these conditions—it would be better to call them states: e.g., God-man, Redeemer, Adorer, but before he was any of these, from eternity, he is the Son. Son is the only way in which he differs from Father and Spirit. Because he is Son he is God-man, Redeemer, Adorer. So union with him in the "whole Christ" is first union with his Sonship, which, in our case, means adoption.

Adoption is not just an accidental result of our being in the "whole Christ," but first in God's intentions for us. This has been said already, but like other apparently separate elements which have been and will be discussed in this book, it must be brought in again and related to other points, to demonstrate the amazing unity of Christian dogma and hence to facilitate Christian life. Yes, just as Christ's basic state is that of Son, so is ours: "...God sent his Son...that we might receive the adoption."[3] First we are sons, then all the rest, as we shall see.

If we are sons we must act toward the Father as his sons. Our new condition is not only an attitude but a whole way of life. There is a principle of philosophy that states, "Action follows being." When we considered nature this principle was pretty well clarified: because a thing possesses a certain nature it acts in a certain way. No act that is foreign to a nature can proceed from that nature. If a dog talks it is not because of his canine nature. Either there is a ventriloquist in the vicinity or we are faced with the phenomenon of a man-dog. Hence, since God wills us to be his adopted sons and to act as such, he has given us with sonship a new nature.

In a family there can be three kinds of sons: natural, adopted, and foster. The foster son is not strictly a member of the family, he has no rights deriving from his condition. In reality he is a guest, yet without a guest's privileges. A foster child has to "toe the line" or else the family gets rid of him. Not so the adopted son. He is truly a son of the adopting parents in every way with only one exception—he is not their natural child. But they have made up for this by giving him, as far as possible, their nature—*so that* he can in every way act as their natural child.

This is exactly what happens in the God-to-man relationship we have been discussing. In adopting us as true adopted sons—"...and if a son, an heir also through God's grace"[4]—the Father gives us, as far as this is possible, his nature, so that we can in every way act as his Son. This new nature is what theology calls *sanctifying,* or *created,* grace. As in the case of the nature which the adopting parents give the child, this cannot be the same nature as God's, or else we would be the natural Son, but similar to it. As in human adoption this bestowed nature is a basis for acting.

We know that the Son-made-man merited adoption for us by his redemptive death, and that we are adopted by our organic union with him, with his Mystical Body. Therefore this new nature that enables us to act as sons is given to us through the Son as its meritorious cause, and in the Son. We can conclude, then, that sanctifying grace is the divine nature created for us by Christ, given to us by our union with him, so that we can act as the Son. What we get is not simply the created share in God's nature-in-general, as did Adam, but that nature coming to us through and in the Son so that we can be, as far as that is possible to creatures, the Son. In short, sanctifying grace is dynamic adopted Sonship.

This is why in our diagram the procedure was Father → Son → Spirit → Son, not Spirit → sons. By our union with Christ we are to be the Son to the Father.

Adopted sonship is the result of God's giving himself to us: the Father gives himself to us in giving us his Son as God-man and Redeemer. Both give us the Spirit, who personally comes to each one at baptism; and at the instant of our union with Christ, he gives himself to us to be our new life. All the good things that are the "fullness" of Christ the Holy Spirit first gives us in giving himself. The *Veni Creator* calls him the "gift of the most high God," and St. Paul writes: "...God's love is poured forth in our hearts by the Holy Spirit who has been given us."[5]

> Grace is...not a thing: it is, on God's side, the gift of God *communicating Himself to man,* and, on man's side, the transformation of his person in response to *the new presence of God,* a transformation in which he is configured to Christ in whose grace and in whose response to God he now participates.[6]

Grace is, then, in the logical order, the result of the presence within us of God giving us himself.[7]

In practice, living our adopted sonship is living the life of the Son. First of all, the Spirit of the Son is within us, enabling us to enter upon a personal relationship with God the Father.[8] Second, he puts us in contact with the entire life of the Son. As the Trinitarian role of the Son is glory—giving the Father the glory of being his image, and of love—so now this twofold glory is the driving force in our life. Since the Son is the image of the Father—"He who sees me sees the Father"[9]—the Son becomes for us way, truth, and life. The Spirit forms us into his image, and is himself our love.

Fortunately for us humans the Son became one of us. Hence as man he was the perfect image of the Father. And this image is something concrete, that our imagination can grasp: acts, words, sufferings, silences. We watch Christ in the Gospels making every human act a perfect concrete image of the divine nature, and giving his Father the glory of love—the union of his human will with the divine.

But our response is not imitation. It can't be, for imitation supposes that we are outside of the one we are imitating. For example, when a small boy has seen a Western movie he consciously works at the peculiar walk of his hero, tilts his cowboy hat, talks, and even spits the same way. He is *imitating,* because he is *exterior* to his hero: there is the hero, on the screen; here is the small boy, in the seat. The boy looks, listens, and imitates. But we are not exterior to Christ; we are *in* him, in the "whole Christ." We share the same life with him. Therefore Christ must live his life in and through us.

> Here...identification with our Savior brings with it a communication of life. "I live now not I, but Christ liveth in me. (Gal 2:20). Our life is not added to Christ's—it is his to such a point that he is the subject of it. We can gauge how far St. Paul extends Christ's possession of us by the fact that he attributes our life to him, not because of our Lord's supernatural universal causality, but because he is the subject of it: "I live now not I, but Christ liveth in me." "Strange though such a teaching may seem, hard though it may appear to reconcile it with the absolute distinctness of Christ and the Christian, St. Paul does, without doubt, say, 'It is Christ who lives in me.'" Christ superimposes his own personality on ours; our Christian being and our life belong to him before belonging to us, he "identifies our new self with him."[10]

Each baptism is for Christ a new Incarnation, for the Christian life means that the baptized must relive and continue Christ's earthly life. He reads the Gospels to see what this life is, but fundamentally the process is not so much imitation as a mutual participation: we sharing in Christ's life, he acting through ours. This does not destroy our personality. In fact Christ uses us as individuals to reach other individuals, who will be more effectively drawn to him through us. And certainly if Christ is to live, not we, whatever there is in us of sin and fault must go, must give way to him. We shall discuss all of this more particularly when treating of the sacraments in detail.

Suffice it to say now that with the divine life the Spirit gives us the seven infused virtues and the seven gifts, means of forming us into Christ's image. You will recall that the virtues are the three theological—faith, hope, and charity—and the four moral—prudence, justice, fortitude, and temperance. While these are called virtues, they are not habits we develop on our own, but rather infused, poured in, powers to perform acts of these virtues. All seven must, if the power is to be operative by the Spirit, be performed for love of God, for their end is formation into Christ, living as the incarnate Son. The gifts—fear of God, piety, fortitude, counsel, knowledge, understanding, and wisdom—are also powers, enabling us to "catch" particular inspirations of the Spirit that, again, would form us into the image of Christ.

We must also, and chiefly, give the Father the glory of love. Shocking as this may seem, the love that the Father wants from us is not so much our own love but the love that the Son gives him. What is this love? It is the Spirit. St. Paul emphatically expressed this: "God's love is poured forth in our hearts by the Holy Spirit who has been given us." And in our hearts the Son by means of the Spirit cries out in love, "Abba! Father!" "Thus dost Thou make us love Thee; or rather, it is thus that Thou lovest Thyself in us."[11] We must love, of course, but even our own love is the result of infused charity; it is ours, therefore, by courtesy of the Holy Spirit. The Spirit takes our love and joins it to divine love, which is himself. "We love God through God, and all supernatural love constitutes, so to speak, one God, loving Himself in Jesus Christ."[12]

While the Mystical Body is still "catching up" with the earthly life of its head, that head is in his glory, at the "right hand" of the Father. Our head is in heaven, and so, in a way, are we. "I come from the Father and have come into the world. And now I am leaving the world and going home to the Father."[13] Christ's cycle is now complete, and eventually we, too, who are at present in the world shall leave it to go home to the Father. Christ is there incomplete, waiting for his whole body. Also he is there as a pledge, that where the Son by nature is, there also shall be the adopted sons. "He has placed at the right hand of your glory the substance of our frailty united to him."[14] If he is there, we surely shall follow; "...and if a son, an heir also...."

But what shall we do in heaven? If we are to live every day with our sight set on Christ in glory, seeking "...the things that are above, where Christ is seated at the right hand of God,"[15] our minds should be as clear as possible as to our occupation in heaven. A hazy goal makes for mighty hazy motivation. Surely twanging a lyre for all eternity is not much inducement to leave forever gracious suburban living.

Our goal, as we do know, is the beatific vision. I have mentioned this term a number of times in the first chapter, where we discussed the fact that everyone is on the supernatural level, at least as to his end—the beatific vision. I mentioned, too, the "image of God" in Adam, which was sanctifying grace. These two terms, which express the most important realities in our life, namely, our goal and our means to it, have become cliché, and, like all clichés, have lost meaning. We have considered grace, now let's look at the beatific vision.

The term itself is a metaphor—we cannot see the divine nature—which means knowing God *as he is.* "We know that when he appears, we shall be like him, because we shall see him just as he is."[16] "We see now by means of a mirror in a vague way, but then we shall see face to face. Now my knowledge is incomplete, but then I shall have complete knowledge, even as God has complete knowledge of me."[17] The tremendous thing about the beatific vision is that we will be able to know the unknowable divine nature. That which we can know now only *by means of* something else, such as revelation, we shall know without any means, directly. There will not even be an *idea* of God in our intellect. He will unite himself directly to our intellect and we shall know him through this union. And to know God *as he is,* is really something that only God can do, just as knowing ourselves as we are is something that even spouses and best friends can't do—or even psychiatrists.

If we are to know as God knows, God must give us a share in his nature—action proceeds from nature—which is precisely what God has already done, years ago, in fact. Yes—we are back to sanctifying grace again! Grace, then, is essentially the same thing as the beatific vision, as the acorn is essentially the oak, and the baby, the man.[18] Another reason for living every day with our eyes on Christ in glory. We are halfway there already.

But what of the glory of love? The beatific vision implies love, for whom, knowing God as he is, can fail to love him? Who will ever be able to turn away from that vision and fail to love? No, such knowledge will be the foundation of beatific love, and eternal giving of self to him who is.

We are ready to study the sacraments, but before we do, it might help if we tie everything together. God created us in his image and therefore we are on the supernatural level. Each one has the spirit, which is the capability for supernatural union with God. The Son became man and restored the image. But since we receive the divine life through and in him, we become one with him, and therefore adopted sons. The image of our re-creation is that of the Son. Our spirit is oriented to union, first with the Son, and second, in him, with the Father—both to be realized perfectly and permanently in the beatific vision. The work of union is the activity of the Spirit. The mutual acts—God's and ours—by which this union is achieved are the sacraments.

Notes

1. Col 1:18-20.
2. This cannot be a mere acceptance of Christ as our Savior. Cf. Alfred Wikenhauser, *Pauline Mysticism* (New York: Herder and Herder, 1960), pp. 92-95.
3. Gal 4:4-5.
4. Gal 4:7.
5. Rom 5:5.
6. Matthew O'Connell, S.J., "The Sacraments in Theology Today," *Thought,* Vol. 36, No. 140, 1961, p. 45.
7. Cf. Karl Rahner, S.J., *Theological Investigations* (Baltimore: Helicon Press, 1961), Vol. I, pp. 320-325.
8. This is the meaning of Rom 8:14-16.

9.   Jn 14:9.

10.   F.X. Durrwell, *The Resurrection* (New York: Sheed and Ward, 1962), pp. 211-212. The quotations are from L. Malavez, *L'Eglise Corps du Christ,* pp. 64, 62.

11.   William of St. Thierry, in Émile Mersch, S.J., *The Whole Christ* (Milwaukee: The Bruce Publishing Company, 1938), p. 445.

12.   Mersch, *op. cit.,* p. 446.

13.   Jn 16:28.

14.   *Communicantes* for the feast of the Ascension.

15.   Col 3:1.

16.   1 Jn 3:2.

17.   1 Cor 13:12.

18.   Cf. St. Thomas, *Summa Contra Gentiles,* chs. 51 and 52.

SEVEN

The Sacraments: Acts

We must stop thinking of the sacraments as things: they are acts, God's and ours. Fr. O'Connell, S.J., has provided an accurate, as well as moving, definition:

> ...[W]e might describe a Christian sacrament as a symbolic action whereby Christ continues in and through His Church the perfect cult of His earthly mysteries and whereby He sanctifies His members, configuring them to Himself and by that very fact dynamically ordering them to the fulfillment of salvation in the vision of God.[1]

The essence of this definition is the term *symbolic action,* for there is this to note about a sacrament—the action cannot be taken on its face value; it only symbolizes the hidden reality that it contains. The apparent action of baptism is a washing, but the action that is really happening is the great act of God whereby the Spirit unites the person with the Son, and the Father welcomes him as an adopted son. Under cover of the symbolic action God comes to man and man comes to God.

> To say that a sacrament is a gift of God is true but it is not enough. It is also a step taken by man as he goes to meet this gift; it is this very meeting. It is not only an initiative, a call on God's part, it is also man's response, or rather it is this very dialogue.[2]

It takes two to make a sacramental act—the priest is only God's human agent—the Caller and the called, and the latter must respond. Fr. DeLetter, S.J., writes:

> ...[T]o the action of Christ coming to meet us in the sacraments must correspond on our part our own going to meet Him, by our desire and readiness or proper dispositions to accept His grace.[3]

Where God acts, there he is present, for his presence cannot be separated from his activity. Think of the presence of God in the confessional! This is a consoling, and fortifying, thought for the confessor as well as for the penitent. We tend to think of the presence of God, say, in the Blessed Sacrament or in the person in grace, as something static, inactive. He is present for our consolation. Yes, but even more is he present for activity, for changing us into himself. The presence of God is always dynamic. Even more in the sacramental moments. These are like the great visitations of God to his people in the Old Testament, always under cover of some symbolic action.

"And all Mount Sinai was on a smoke: because the Lord was come down upon it in fire, and the smoke arose from it as out of a furnace: and all the Mount was terrible." "And the sight of the glory of the Lord was like a burning fire upon the top of the Mount, in the eyes of the children of Israel."⁴ The sacraments are the great visitations of God in the New Testament, and because they occur so frequently—daily Communions, weekly confessions—we fail to see them as great. But under the symbolic actions of eating, of rendering a judgment, to name only two, God comes down to our mountain, and, unlike the children of Israel, we are not only able, but invited, to come up to him.

Although the biblical definition of God is "He who is," we realize from the Bible that God also is "He who acts." For God *is* act, and his activity, because of creation and re-creation, flows into creation, which only exists because of the act of God. Let us look at Chapter 5 of St. John's Gospel for evidences of God's activity. "My Father," Jesus said, "has been working to this hour, and so I, too, am working."

> I tell you the plain truth: the Son can do nothing on his own initiative; he can only do what he sees the Father do. Yes, what he is doing—that, and nothing else, the Son does likewise. The Father dearly loves the Son, and lets him see everything he himself is doing; in fact, he will let him see even greater exercises of power than the ones you witnessed, so that you will be astonished. For example, just as the Father raises the dead and gives them life, so, too, does the Son give life to anyone he

> chooses. Nor, again, does the Father judge
> anyone; no, the right to judge he has turned
> over wholly to the Son.[5]

The act of God is daily giving life in baptism, and destroying sin in the sacrament of penance.

The sacraments are the means by which we relive and continue Christ's life; they put us in contact with his earthly acts. Baptism is the initial contact; from then on the contact progresses and intensifies. Thus the sacraments give us Christ's acts that they may become our acts. Thus he progressively reveals himself to us through the sacraments.

Now that we have considered some basic notions of the sacraments, let us dig in—in earnest. A sacrament is a symbolic action, instituted by Christ, to give grace. There must be present two distinct elements: the natural and the supernatural. The natural element may be bread, eaten by a human being, or it may be oil, applied to a body, or words—created thought symbols. But this element alone would be meaningless. Bread is eaten, oil is applied, words are said, every day, but these actions are in themselves not sacraments. The supernatural must be present to shape them as sacraments or give them form. Granted their institution by Christ, the sacramental actions are only sacramental because Christ uses them to give the divine life of adopted sonship that is in him in its fullness, as well as the infused virtues, gifts, and special actual grace. We can say, then, that it is the intention of Christ that gives these actions their meaning as sacraments.

We are reminded here of Christ himself. His human nature conceals his divine; the Person of the Son is present in the humanity of him who, since the Incarnation, is named Jesus. And since the resurrection the divine life of the Son has in every way made its influence felt in his human life. Adoption was merited for us by his human nature, but the redemptive act acquired meaning only by reason of the intention of the Son. Adoption, and all that Christ merited, are conveyed to man by means of his human nature, for the sacraments are, as I have said, contacts with the humanity of Christ, with his acts. Thus Christ is the first sacrament.[6]

But Christ is sacrament as God-man by the fact of the Incarnation. His created human nature is man's contact with God. God becomes visible and audible, concrete, human, and appealing, for an initial man-to-man relationship that leads into one that is man-to-God. The Word became man so that man might become the Word adoptively. His sacramental humanity conceals God, and since the resurrection "we have looked upon his glory— such a glory as befits the Father's only-begotten Son— full of grace and truth!"[7] Without the human nature we could not look upon God. But now it becomes the place of meeting him; Christ is the mediator of this encounter.[8]

The incarnate Word is also the meeting place for all creation. Having a body, he has kinship with the mineral, vegetable, and animal kingdoms; having a soul, with the angels. But it is the risen Christ who, mysteriously and wonderfully, takes creation into his Mystical Body. "And this good pleasure he decreed to put into effect in Christ when the designated period of time had elapsed, namely to gather all creation both in heaven and on earth under one head, Christ."[9] This happens now by the Christian's use of creation: when he sees it as the Son sees it—"All things came into being through him"[10]—and uses it as the Son would. The Christian becomes Christ's touch upon creation, and by this touch the creature is able to fulfill its Creator's purpose. It returns to him through the mediation of the Christian, who is the extension in creation of Christ's human nature. But its union with Christ will be fully realized at his second coming, when "...we look for new heavens and a new earth, in which holiness dwells."[11]

But Christ is the first sacrament not only as being God-man, but especially as Redeemer, whereby he is the source of grace and gives it. I would like to expand now the introductory remarks I made about Christ as sacrament. Christ merited sonship for us, as well as its concomitant graces, by means of his human nature. Each act of Christ, however insignificant, was in some way a source of sonship for us. For example, an act of obedience to the Blessed Mother merited obedience and humility for us, not just the grace to be obedient and humble, but a participation in these virtues in him who would be our head and the chief principle of our actions. Thus we might be able to give lawful authority not just our obedience, but the humble obedience of the incarnate Son, obeying through it his Father's will. Actual adopted sonship he merited by his death, and at his resurrection his whole Person was one source of sonship to be given. It is given when the sacramental action occurs. Christ himself is sacramental, because he not only creates, but also gives the grace. "The sacraments are acts of Christ."[12]

But there is something missing here. If a sacrament is essentially a symbolic action, how can Christ be a sacrament just because he gives grace by means of symbolic actions performed by others? He must give it by means of his own. He does, as can be inferred from the preceding paragraph. Every human action by which Christ merited was symbolic because he performed it in order to merit. Thus, when he made a box in his carpenter's shop he was not making a box only in order to make a living. It looked like that, but the apparent action hid the real action that was going on: union of his human will with his Father's will, to give the Father glory and to merit for man. Why else should *Christ* be making a box? So his death was not merely a death; it very definitely was the symbolic atoning death of the whole human race.

But these symbolic actions *merited* grace, and a sacrament contains and *conveys* it. The acts of Christ that he performed then are the means by which he gives grace *now*. Since sonship was merited essentially by his death, every sacrament has to be radically a participation in that death. Christ died *for* us, therefore we were there, we of the present, dying in him and with him. It only wanted two things: for us to exist in time and for us to be united to him. We entered him through union with his death. "Surely," St. Paul wrote to the Romans, "if when we were enemies we were reconciled to God by the death of his Son, much more, once we are reconciled, shall we be saved by his life."[13] Yes, Christ reconciled us to God, saved us, then, but what good to us was the reconciliation, the salvation, unless it can come to us now? It does, now, in the sacraments. Thus the symbolic action of Christ's death is the basic sacramental action, for it is, essentially, the source of grace. Whenever a sacramental action is happening, the dying of Christ is present, for without that dying the sacrament would be meaningless.

With reference to the *then* and *now* aspect of Christ's actions, St. Paul wrote: "With Christ I am nailed to the cross."[14] Dom Odo Casel thus commented on this passage: "Here the master and the pupil are put wholly into the same point of time; both hang together on the same cross. They have become contemporaries in every detail. Yet from that it follows that Christ, although he is in glory with the Father, hangs on a cross for the Church, and not merely *has* hung there…."[15] But how can this be? Christ's earthly acts are over. How can his dying be made present if a sacrament is to have value, and how can we contact his other symbolic actions, now past? Christ's human acts are over, it is true, as to their execution. They are now historical acts. But because they were symbolic, performed in order to merit, they do remain in Christ as sources of the grace merited. They are present in him *by reason of their power*. Each one, then, is an outward sign that is a storehouse of potential adopted sonship, and by contacting them in the sacraments we contact their power. So Christ's actions are truly sacramental, and when a sacrament is given, they are brought forward to us in time. Christ is the first-sacrament because his symbolic actions are active by their effects in the sacraments.

You will notice that I have called the human acts of Christ storehouses of adopted sonship, for their purpose—and, therefore, that of the sacraments—is to make us be by grace what the Son is by nature. We do not *imitate* Christ, we must *be* Christ. As Fr. Davis has well said:

> ...[W]e are Christians only because there is realized in us what was realized in Christ. The mystery of Christ extends also to us and embraces us, so that we not merely receive grace from the saving work of Christ, but also enter into that work itself.... The saving mystery of Christ is rendered present in the liturgy in the sense that, in the liturgy, what was done in Christ is done in us by the action of Christ.[16]

Chiefly through the sacraments are we able to carry out our part of the Mystical Body—to relive and continue the earthly life of our head.

The source of grace is there, in the glorified, ascended Christ, until human agents perform the sacramental action. Then Christ takes over the action, by his intention and his giving, which become the very heart of the symbolic action. The latter is enacted by the human agents, e.g., confessor and penitent, but is only the means by which the real action is set in motion. We must not think that Christ makes a new intention every time a sacrament is performed. The intention is once and for all in the risen Christ to give grace. It is the symbolic action that makes his intention operative.[17]

But the human agents do not act as private individuals. Their action is not only that of Christ, but also that of the Church. "Therefore the Church may herself be called a primal sacrament, inasmuch as she is the 'sacramental Christ' and the recipient of the seven sacraments."[18] Up to now my emphasis has been on the relation of Christ to the individual, but it is time that we see the individual in his relation to the other members of the Mystical Body, in other words, it is time that we consider the Church.

The Church *is* the Mystical Body, therefore it is one with the head; the members are one with each other—one organic whole. As such the Church is a sacrament, for very definitely is it *the* outward sign instituted by Christ to give grace. It has its created, visible element—people—ordinary and extraordinary people, human, weak, good, and bad, every possible variety. It has its invisible element—Christ and, in him, the Father and the Spirit. The people—the "outward signs"—act symbolically, sacramentally, and God acts. This interaction is the essential life of the Church.

The ascended Christ today acts in and through the Church; he is dynamic, as he was when visibly present, but his influence now flows from him within the Church to his members, who must make the unseen reality visible, concrete, in themselves, and let the influence of Christ contact those whom he wishes to, by means of their contact.

Christ made his revelation, not to individuals, but first to the Church. He decreed the sacraments to the Church; therefore it is in the Church that we look for the sacraments, for their number, specific differences, performance. And because the Church is the visible, tangible, and audible Christ, with one human person to be his vicar, with actual human representatives of the Apostles, we look to it for the sacramental moments that will unlock for us the activity of Christ. We can meditate by ourselves on Christ's acts as we read of them in the Gospels and hope in his love and mercy for the grace that these merited, but when the Church sacramentally puts us in organic contact with these acts, we *know* that we are receiving the grace merited. And since the purpose of the Church is to bring us to the beatific vision, through, in, and with the incarnate Son, the sacraments are the essential life of the Church; there can be no other.

Therefore, the sacraments reveal the Church, what it basically is, what precisely forms its purpose. This private devotions cannot do, and don't pretend to do. But at times private devotions can hide the essential life of the Church, and the losers are those who are not living by their main sources. Of this we are sure, where the sacraments are, there has to be the Church. As visible signs, the sacraments reveal the Church by making it recognizable. If an element of one of these signs is changed, it must be changed by the Church.

"But to each one of us grace has been given to the extent to which Christ imparts it,"[19] St. Paul wrote, and from this principle he concluded as to the different degrees in the Church. The degrees result from Christ's grace given in the sacraments; it establishes hierarchy, from baptism to holy orders. It "structures" the Church as to function and to state. A true society must have interrelationships, which themselves create differences in degree. In the Church these relationships are created by the sacraments, which, then, confer specific vocations. This we shall see later in more detail.

The Church relives and continues the life of Christ. He uses the Church to give his redemption through the sacraments, but he also, and primarily, uses it to give the Father glory. Whenever a sacrament occurs in the Church the original symbolic action of Christ is made present through its effects. Its first effect is glory to the Father. "I have glorified you on earth by completing the work you gave me to do."[20]

We must not forget that Christ's human nature, although God because united to the Person of the Son, is a *created* nature, therefore it has the obligation of worship. Christ's human nature adores the divine by means of its human intellect and will, acknowledging thereby that God is its creator. Adoration is the most basic form of glory that a human person can give to God, because it tells him that the creature has grasped the fundamental difference between God and himself: God is being from himself, the creature is being from God. Adoration is expressed by some external act, and that act is worship.

Every human act that Christ performed was worship, for it proceeded from his adoration—from his realization as man of his creatureship, and of the necessity of uniting his human will to the divine.

So when the Church performs a sacrament, Christ worships the Father, for the sacrament makes present his fundamental disposition of adoration that made the represented action a symbol of worship in the first place.

And thus the Church worships the Father through its head. Christ is the way, the mediator; and the way to the Father is not direct, but *through* Christ. The Church can never pray alone, its worship can never be exclusively the worship of the Church. It has to be the worship of Christ, to which the Church joins its own. Christ worships for the Church whenever it makes present his actions, symbolic of worship, in the sacraments.

Because he is the first sacrament Christ is the priest for the Church. He performs the function of middleman, between the Father and the Church, mediating our worship and love through his own.

Notes

1. Matthew O'Connell, S.J., "The Sacraments in Theology Today," *Thought,* 1961, Vol. No. 36, p. 45.
2. A.M. Roguet, O.P., *The Sacraments: Signs of Life* (London: Blackfriars, 1954), p. 27.
3. P. DeLetter, S.J., "The Encounter with God," *Thought,* 1961, Vol. No. 36, p. 11. Cf. Edward H. Schillebeeckx, O.P., "The Sacraments: An Encounter with God," *Theology Digest,* 1960, pp. 112-121.
4. Ex 19:18; 24:17 (Douay-Rheims version).
5. Jn 5:17, 19-22.

6.   Cf. Edward H. Schillebeeckx, O.P., *Christ the Sacrament of the Encounter with God* (New York: Sheed and Ward, 1963), pp. 7-47.

7.   Jn 1:14.

8.   Cf. Thomas W. Heaney, "A Personalist Approach to Symbol and Sacrament," *The Feehan Review,* Spring, 1963, pp. 11-12.

9.   Eph 1:10.

10.   Jn 1:3.

11.   Cf. Rom 8:19-22; 2 Pt 3:13.

12.   *Directoire pour la Pastorale des Sacrements,* quoted by Roguet, *op. cit.,* p. 11.

13.   Rom 5:10. Read Chapter 6 of Romans.

14.   Gal 2:20.

15.   Odo Casel, O.S.B., *The Mystery of Christian Worship* (Westminster, Md.: The Newman Press, 1962), p. 155.

16.   Charles Davis, *Liturgy and Doctrine* (New York: Sheed and Ward, 1960), pp. 82-83. The whole book would be helpful. Fr. Davis's use of the word *liturgy* here reminds us that the sacraments comprise the most important of the liturgy.

17.   Cf. *Summa Theologiae,* III, Q. 62,. art. 4; Q. 66, art. 2.

18.   Schillebeeckx, *loc. cit.,* p. 119.

19.   Eph 4:7.

20.   Jn 17:4.

EIGHT

The Sacraments: Signs

A sacrament is basically a symbolic action that makes present an action of Christ, in order to give us the grace of adopted sonship. The *relationship* between the two actions constitutes the substance of a sacrament. Catholics become scandalized when they read that at one time the Western Church conferred confirmation only by the imposition of the bishop's hand, and later borrowed the use of chrism from the Eastern Church. Did not Christ, they ask, determine the matter and form to be used in the sacraments? Not necessarily. What Christ determined essentially was that there should be seven symbolic actions, whose symbolism would be related to the grace being given. As Fr. Camelot wrote recently: "…the essential element of a sacrament [is] its relation to the reality signified."[1]

We can better understand this when we realize that the sacraments are signs and what that means. A sign is a way of knowing something through at least one of the senses. When we see smoke we know that there is fire; when we hear a birdcall we know that a bird is in the offing. We hear or read words and know facts or ideas. Signs can be either natural or arbitrary. The smoke and the birdcall proceed naturally from their source, but language does not—it is strictly arbitrary, like barber poles and the old-fashioned vases of colored water in a druggist's window.

The sacraments are arbitrary signs. They are ways of knowing that grace is dynamically present. God could certainly have given grace without them—directly from him to the soul, bypassing the body—but he did not. He chose a means of grace suited to us as human beings, employing the activity of the body as well as of the soul. And therefore he decreed that his grace be given by means of signs. The fact that he was giving grace had to be apparent to at least one of the senses. So when we say that Christ established the seven sacraments we do not say that he determined precisely what the signs should be, but that there should be signs—grace through signs. As a fact he did prescribe those for baptism and Eucharist, but underlying this prescription was the wonderful fact that he was going to give his grace by means of symbolic actions.

While he was visibly present on earth, Christ operated through signs. What else were his miracles but ways for the people to know that God's power was present and active? St. John in the sixth chapter of his Gospel uses the Greek word for *sign* several times.

Fr. Kleist translates it as *miracle* in verses 2 and 14, *manifestations of power* in verse 26, and *proofs of your claims* in verse 30.[2] These are three shades of the same meaning: that Christ's miracles are signs, manifesting his power to the intellect by means of sense knowledge. We recall the signs by which the Jews knew God's love and mercy, his mind and plans in their regard, during the years of the Exodus: the pillar of fire, the luminous cloud, the brazen serpent, the stone tablets with the Ten Commandments. Until he unites his essence directly to our intellects in the beatific vision, God's way of encountering us is by signs. Christ's human nature is the greatest of these.

God's signs are his method of showing us the unseen, something of himself. So the sacraments give us God in adopted sonship, which in itself gives us God. St. Thomas says: "Consequently a sacrament is a sign that is both a reminder of the past, i.e., the passion of Christ, and an indication of that which is effected in us by Christ's passion, i.e., grace; and a prognostic, that is, a foretelling of future glory."[3]

> Every sacrament, then, has something to declare: it recalls the past, it is the voice of the present, it reveals the future. If the sacrament did not fulfill its function of sign proclaiming something that is not seen, it would not be a sacrament at all. It can embrace heaven and earth, time and eternity, because it is a sign; were it only a grace it would be no more than the gift of the present hour; but being a sign the whole history of the spiritual

> world is reflected in it: "For as often as you
> shall eat this bread and drink the chalice, you
> shall show the death of the Lord, until He
> come" (1 Cor 11:26).[4]

In the sacraments God conveys to us the invisible through that which is apparent to our senses "...while we direct our gaze not at what is seen but at what is unseen. What we see is temporary, but what we do not see endures forever."[5] Hence in every sacrament there are bodily and other material elements, following the pattern of the first sacrament, the Word-made-flesh. Inherent in our European culture is an uncomfortable feeling about matter. While we don't consider it to be evil, we are apt, at least unconsciously, to think of it as the source of evil. St. Cyril of Jerusalem was quite of the contrary notion:

> Tell me not that the body is a cause of sin. For
> if the body is a cause of sin, why does not a
> dead body sin? ...The body sins not of itself,
> but the soul through the body. The body is an
> instrument, and, as it were, a garment and
> robe of the soul: and if by this latter it be
> given over to fornication, it becomes defiled:
> but if it dwell with a holy soul, it becomes a
> temple of the Holy Ghost.[6]

Tertullian, the apologist, wrote in about the year 211:

> The body plays a vital role in salvation. For
> when the soul is dedicated to God, it is the
> body that makes this possible. The body is
> washed that the soul might be cleansed; the

> body is anointed that the soul might be conse-
> crated; the body is sealed and the soul is
> fortified; the body is overshadowed by the
> imposition of hands and the soul is illumi-
> nated by the Spirit; the body partakes of the
> body and blood of Christ, and the soul gets
> fat on God. They cannot be separated from
> the reward, whom these actions unite.[7]

Our downgrading matter comes to us chiefly from the
Greek philosopher, Plato, and the man who sparked neo-
Platonism in the Christian era, Plotinus. To these men
there was something degenerate about anything created,
especially material creation. The body as the prison of
the soul is a Platonic concept. The biblical concept of
matter is something entirely different. In fact, one of the
reasons for the Genesis account of creation is to show
that God created matter, and that, therefore, it is good.
"And God saw all the things that he had made, and they
were very good."[8] It is a great loss to Catholic spirituality that to a certain degree Platonism affected some of its
influential writers. How much healthier Christian life
would be today if our writers had all had a biblical mentality. What a greater appreciation we would have of the
sacraments, which give the spiritual by means of the
material.

The Old Testament abounds in the signs by
which God contacted his people. These were concrete,
rather than abstract; even God's most solemn word-signs
were given from out of some matter-sign, such as thun-
der, clouds, fire, and trumpet blasts. The whole Old
Testament is a sign in itself: the people of God. The sign

embraced the past (the main reason for the Genesis account of creation), established the proper relation with God for their present, and looked forward to fulfillment in the Mystical Body. The covenant and the exodus became the great directing and sustaining signs for the people of God.

Let us look briefly at the covenant. God said to Abraham: "And I will establish my covenant between me and thee, and between thy seed after thee in their generations, by a perpetual covenant: to be a God to thee, and to thy seed after thee." This in itself was a sign, but its meaning was not fully revealed until the New Testament. St. Paul has given it to us: "To Abraham were the promises made and to his seed. He saith not, *And to his seeds,* as of many: but as of one, *And to his seed,* which is Christ."[9] Christ, the great and primary sign of the New Testament, is the fulfillment of that of the Old. He is the head of the people of God, who form his body. Because he is the completion of the covenant, the messianic signs fit into the larger one.

The covenant became manifest through another sign, circumcision. "This is my covenant which you shall keep, between you and me and your descendants after you: Every male among you shall be circumcised." St. Paul underscored the meaning of this sign that the Jews should have understood from its relation to Abraham: "He [Abraham] received circumcision as the seal of the holiness which comes from faith. He had this holiness before he was circumcised, that he might be the father of all who believe, even though uncircumcised, and thus have their faith credited to them as holiness."[10] This sign indicated that God had given holiness to Abraham because he first believed.

The exodus is another major sign of the Old Testament, a beloved period in their history that the Jews were fond of recalling. To the prophets the exodus was the time of Israel's communion with God and dependence upon him, of God's loving care for his people. It was kept alive in the great feasts, especially the most solemn of all, the Passover. The exodus was not merely a past event, but a pledge of God's protection and a promise of future Passovers, and its signs formed the pattern of the Jew's spiritual life.[11]

The sign value of the paschal meal in the mind of contemporary American Jews can be seen in these words of Rabbi Martin Berkowitz:

> Passover proclaims an eternal message, not one restricted to an eight-day period. It is concerned with a universal concept, not one limited to a single people.... The Jewish family, by concerning itself with the wider application of the Passover message, sees the direct relevance of its religious heritage to the modern struggle for a better world and a finer humanity.[12]

While this interpretation is not strictly messianic in the traditional sense, it illustrates the fact that the sign concept is inherent in biblical religion, and therefore spirituality.

The sign of the paschal meal found its fulfillment in the sign of the Eucharist. Christ established this sacrament in the framework of the paschal meal; the bread he used was the prescribed matzoth, which at one point of the meal had to be broken and distributed; the wine that Christ consecrated was that drunk at the end of the meal. The grace he said before each consecration was, no doubt, the psalms that formed part of the ritual. Christ's use of elements of the paschal meal for the Eucharist was not an accidental thing, nor was his choice of these merely based on their suitability. No, in using these elements, in the progress of the paschal meal, he showed the true and ultimate meaning of this Old Testament sign. "It has been my heart's desire," he said to them, "to eat this paschal supper with you before I suffer. I tell you, I shall not eat it again till it is fulfilled in the kingdom of God."[13] The meaning of the paschal meal as a sign is God's covenant with his people, which is fully realized by the kingdom of God through the covenant-blood of Christ.[14]

Another exodus sign, which was fulfilled only by the Eucharist, was the manna. "This is the bread which the Lord has given you to eat," Moses told the Jews on the morning the manna first appeared. "I tell you the plain truth," replied Jesus, "Moses did not give you the bread from heaven; not at all: my Father gives you the real bread from heaven; for only the bread that comes down from heaven for the purpose of giving life to the world is God's bread."[15]

Christ's designation of water as the sign for baptism—"born of water and the Spirit"—apart from its obvious relation to cleansing, recalls the passage of the Jews through the sea: "When the water was thus divided, the Israelites marched into the midst of the sea on dry land, with the water like a wall to their right and to their left." The deluge, as an agent of God's purification, also comes to mind, and before that, before the account of creation, the image of "...the spirit of God...stirring above the waters."[16]

The primitive Church turned to the Old Testament for the other sacramental signs. The use of oil, for example, as a sign of consecration had its precedent in the anointing of priests and kings.[17] Christ himself interpreted the meaning of the salt that had to season Old Testament sacrifices when he told the Apostles: "You are the salt of the earth. But suppose salt should lose its savor, what is there to restore its nature?"[18] Thus these signs could embrace the Old Testament preparation, Christ's earthly life, and the eschatological fact—Christ and the Church in glory.[19]

But a sign, because it is a sign, must have meaning. The letters d-o-g taken together mean to the English-speaking a member of the canine family. But a bath of water alone would not mean baptism, but only an action motivated by comfort and charity. It is the intention of Christ that gives a very particular meaning to a particular bath of water, and to all the rest of the sacramental signs. Because Christ intends to give grace by means of this bath of water, this bath becomes baptism.

Christ's intention makes the sacramental sign effective and significant of what it effects.

This intention of Christ is applied to the matter of the sacrament by what theology calls the form. A mere bath cleanses the body, but put a willing catechumen in the bath, add the words, "I baptize you in the name of the Father and of the Son and of the Holy Spirit," and an adopted son of God steps out. The words—or form—make the difference. St. Augustine wrote of this: "The word is joined to the element and the result is a sacrament, itself becoming, in a sense, a visible word as well...."[20]

That is the reason why a sacrament must have matter and form. The action would hardly be symbolic without the words that declare the fact. And in doing so they declare the relationship of this action to the actions of Christ. To repeat and recapitulate: apart from baptism and the Eucharist, Christ did not necessarily determine the matter and form, only that there should be matter and form so that he could give grace by means of signs.

Notes

1.   Pierre-Thomas Camelot, O.P., "Toward a Theology of Confirmation," *Theology Digest,* 1959, p. 69.

2.   Jn 6:2, 14, 26, 30.

3.   *Summa Theologiae,* III, Q. 60, a. 3.

4.   Dom Anscar Vonier, O.S.B., *A Key to the Doctrine of the Eucharist,* in *The Collected Works of Abbot Vonier* (Westminster, Md.: The Newman Press, n.d.), p. 238. Chapters 1 to 6 can be read with profit at this point.

5.   2 Cor 4:18.

6.   *Catechetical Lectures,* 4, 23. In Schaff and Wace, eds., *op. cit.,* Vol. 7.

7.   *De Carnis Resurrectione, P.L.* 2, 806.
8.   Gen 1:31.
9.   Gen 17:7; Gal 3:16 (Douay-Rheims version).
10.   Gen 17:10; Rom 4:11.
11.   Read Chapter 1 of Jacques Guillet's *Themes of the Bible* (Notre Dame, Ind.: Fides Publishers Association, 1961).
12.   Martin Berkowitz, *Haggadah for the American Family* (H. Levitt Publishing Co., 1958), from the Foreword.
13.   Lk 22:15-16.
14.   Cf. Mt 26:28; Mk 14:24.
15.   Ex 16:15; Jn 6:32-33.
16.   Jn 3:5; Ex 14:22; Gen 1:2.
17.   Ex 29:7; 1 Sam 10:1.
18.   Lev 2:13; Mt 5:13; cf. Mk 9:49.
19.   Cf. David M. Stanley, S.J., "The New Testament Doctrine of Baptism," *Theological Studies,* June, 1957, pp. 172–175.
20.   *Tractatus in Joannem,* 80, 3. *P.L.* 35, 1840. In Paul F. Palmer, S.J., ed., Sacraments and Worship (Westminster, Md.: The Newman Press, 1955), p. 87. Cf. *Summa Theologiae,* III, Q. 60, a. 6.

The Sacraments: Grace

From the foregoing we realize that there are two causes of grace in the sacraments: Christ and the sacraments themselves. He is, of course, the principal cause, for he is the source of grace, which flows to us from the symbolic representation of his acts. But the sacraments, too, cause grace because they are the instruments, which Christ uses, and which, as instruments, cause and give grace when they are enacted. Of course, if the recipient is not rightly disposed to receive the sacrament, grace is not given. Every sacrament is an encounter with God that is the result of God's act and ours.

God's act is the giving of himself in grace, for that is the primary purpose of the sacraments. We have looked at sanctifying grace in Chapter 6, but now we must study it as being specifically "sacramental." There arises also the question of other grace—actual grace, the virtues and the gifts, and that mysterious thing, the sacramental character.

I have called sanctifying grace dynamic adopted sonship, and throughout this book have emphasized the fact of adoption. This by no means diminishes the notion of grace but rather delineates what Christian grace precisely is: the basis for our acting toward the Father as not only his sons, but especially as his Son. Therefore Christian grace necessarily has to be, first, a sharing in the one divine nature that is common to all three Persons of the Trinity, created for man essentially by the death of Christ. As such, sanctifying grace "divinizes" the recipient, making him radically capable, after his time of trial, of knowing and loving God *in the same way* in which God does, giving him now a new manner of being and living. It's as if his own human nature is incomplete—which, because of God's purpose in creating man, is really the case—and is completed and fulfilled by this gift of God's nature. Grace, then, lifts a man up to God's life, elevating the drabbest human action to God's level of living, never destroying the person, but rather making him more himself. The man in grace lives by two natures, his own and God's, or, to be more correct, by his own divinized.

If we would leave sanctifying grace at that we would be omitting something essential. Christian grace is sacramental. It is normally given by means of the sacraments, and even when it is not, the implication is that it is impossible to receive the sacraments, say, of baptism or penance. Sanctifying grace is the beatific vision in germ, but Christ categorically said: "I am telling you the plain truth: unless a man is born of water and the Spirit, he cannot enter the Kingdom of God!"[1] Grace is a sharing of God's very life, but Christ said: "What I tell you is the plain truth: unless you eat the flesh of the Son of Man and drink his blood, you have no life in you. He who eats my flesh and drinks my blood is in possession of eternal life...."[2]

Christian grace, then, is received through the sacraments; it is given not only *through* Christ, but also *in* him, and, therefore, it confers adopted sonship and is strictly related to the development of Christ in us. Let us see how this is so. First of all, since sanctifying grace comes to us by means of the sacraments it is sacramental in character. Our grace was merited for us by Christ's human acts and is given when these are made present by means of the symbolic acts of the sacraments. Christ's acts *then* cause the grace *now,* because they are made sacramentally present, *now*.

But that isn't all. Baptism unites us to Christ in such a way that we and the rest of the Church make up one Person with him. When the Church performs a sacrament what is happening is this: the human acts of Christ our head are being made present in us his members in order to give us the ability to relive those acts, at least their interior spirit. The sacraments are the continual presence of Christ's life in the "whole Christ" so that the latter can be and live as the Son. Hence Christian grace, the chief effect of the sacraments, is definitely sacramental in character, for its purpose is to confer basic life of Christ, sonship, in all the phases it assumed in him.

In all the phases it assumed in him—this needs clarification. Remember, there are seven sacraments. We must get over any idea we may have of the sacraments being seven pipelines of grace, and that's all. If this were all we would not need seven, but one. The grace in each is directed to producing in us a particular effect or effects. If the sacraments accomplish what they signify, and their symbolic action is related to certain actions of Christ, this must be so. The grace, which the individual sacrament confers, is influenced by the sacrament. We shall study these particular effects when treating of the separate sacraments, but the underlying principle is this: we are to relive not only acts of Christ insofar as possible, but also, and especially, his states, or abiding conditions. The different sacraments give us certain acts and states to relive. We can illustrate this from the special effect of matrimony: the sacrament gives a couple the state of Christ as head of the Mystical Body, capable, because of his atonement, of adding to its increase. This state of Christ is one phase of his fundamental state of Son: because he was first of all Son, Christ obeyed the Father's will unto death, thus meriting for himself the right to be head of his body, the Church, and meriting its growth. So sacramental grace gives the states and acts of Christ proper to each sacrament for our development as Christ.

Theologians speak of the special grace proper to each sacrament as "sacramental grace," as that which enables the recipient to obtain the purposes of that sacrament. Fr. Mersch has written of this:

> In content and nature, sacramental grace is primarily and essentially sanctifying grace, for it is primarily the grace that makes one a living member of the God-man, and that is what sanctifying grace does. But this sanctifying grace, being a grace of union with Christ and the Church, varies according to the degrees of union and the positions in the Church the several sacraments give.[3]

For example, the effect of holy orders is a union with Christ the priest, a deeper union with the head than that which baptism effects.

But sanctifying grace, although it is the basis for our life as sons-by-adoption, is inactive without actual grace. It is the basis, a new nature; but for deliberate, freely willed actions in accord with this nature we have need of special help each time. By way of illustration, say we decide to read one good book a week. Because we are human we are able to read, but that does not mean we are going to. To maintain our resolution we have to make a deliberate act of the will, and provide for a number of other things, such as time, place, relative quiet. During the reading itself we must repeatedly concentrate. All of these acts take special efforts of the intellect and will. And so it is in our living as the Son. Participation in the divine nature is not enough. All day long we need the special assistance of God for our intellect and will if we are going to soar above the mere natural level of living.

Every sacrament gives, in addition to sanctifying grace, a "title" to all the actual graces that the recipient will need to achieve the effects of that sacrament. In other words, if the sacrament is to be fruitful its sanctifying grace has to be effective, which it cannot be without actual grace. I use "title" here because that is precisely the way actual grace is given at the time a sacrament is conferred. It is a promise of help, of power, for the rest of one's life, but always in relation to the effect of the sacrament. Thus the actual graces that result from matrimony will be different from those resulting from holy orders.

These graces flow to us from the acts of Christ, and come to us sacramentally because of our union with him: "...severed from me, you can do nothing."[4] The acts of Christ cause this power in us as we need it, not only because they have merited it, but also because they actually produce it.[5] Christ's actions, you will recall, are all symbolic, in that they were done *primarily* out of his twofold motive: glory to the Father and redemption for man. They are in him now, although historically past, in their internal content. What he did he merited for us to do, and provided the actual power. Not his miracles, perhaps, but the interior dispositions with which he did them—the love, the obedience, the patience, and all the rest of his virtues. So sacramental actual grace is a result of union with Christ in whom these acts exist by their influence. The symbolic acts of the sacraments make them present.

The seven virtues and the gifts are given in the sacraments along with sanctifying grace, always with the particular ends of the various sacraments in view.[6] They are as necessary as actual grace if the sanctifying grace of a sacrament is to achieve its effect. Therefore they are related and adapted to it.[7] The virtues of hope and fortitude, for example, would acquire a special character in the anointing of the sick; the inspirations of the Holy Spirit would seem more likely to be those of the gifts of piety, fortitude, and knowledge.

"Sacramental grace" is sanctifying grace and the "title" to all necessary actual grace. But certainly the virtues and the gifts are sacramental graces, too, and we must think of them as such, for what they do is to make it possible for us to live as Christ, through, in, and with him, in the various sacramental actions.

However, to live as *Christ* demands something other than grace, some principle that is real and lasting and that can serve as a basis for so living. Sanctifying grace is such a basis for living as the *Son,* considered as a *divine* Person, but from the time of the Incarnation on, the Son has also a *human* nature. What permanent principle is there for our reliving his *human* life? That principle is the Mystical Body. To be more precise, that principle is grace—sanctifying and actual—the virtues and the gifts, and the sacramental character, all given to us in Christ as our head. All this, therefore, is given by the sacraments, especially baptism and the Eucharist.

St. Paul teaches that the Mystical Body is a real, abiding, and physical union with Christ, so that we and he form one body, so that we and he become the "whole Christ." "For example, just as the body is a unit, although it has many members, and all the members of the body, many though they are, form but one body, so too is the Christ."[8] Basically there is a resemblance here between the head of a human body and its members. Just as the head is the source of life for the rest of the body, so Christ is the source of life for the Church. But the Mystical Body means more than that: because he is source and because the will of the Father is that the redeemed be adopted sons in Christ, they and he form one organism. If we are to live as the Son—and the Son is now also a human being—we must be physically united to him, God-man, so as to make with him a single Person. If we are to be Christ-by-adoption, and by an adoption that is real, not a metaphor, then our union with him has to be something real. That it is not metaphorical we can gather from these words of St. Paul: "Are you not aware that your bodies are members of Christ's body? Shall I then take the members of Christ and make them the members of a prostitute? Never!"[9]

United thus to Christ we have a permanent basis for living as Christ, and the actual grace of the sacraments acts upon this basis. Merited by his human acts, it enables us to relive these. But we must not undervalue the role of sanctifying grace in this process. The human nature of Christ is so united to his divine nature that there is in him only the one Person: his Person as Son is his sole agent of action. He performed every human act by means of his divine Person.

Hence, we relive Christ's human acts primarily by means of the created participation of the divine nature that is in us. Otherwise we could not live as *Christ* did, who operated primarily as divine. We can say, then, that sanctifying grace makes it relatively possible for us to be the son as Jesus Christ is the Son.

What is the sacramental *character,* which is given only by baptism, confirmation, and orders? The Church Fathers, such as St. Ephrem and St. Augustine, insist on calling it a "seal" or a "brand," metaphorically, of course, but to us today these figures of speech do not mean much. We do not do much sealing with sealing wax, and we only brand cattle now, no longer soldiers. We thus tend to dismiss the *character* as something that exists, but as something quaint and rather difficult to grasp anyway; hence not too worthy of our consideration. It might be easier if we first look at the sacramental *character* as being a sign of consecration, priesthood, and incorporation.[10]

When something is consecrated it is set aside for the exclusive use of God, it belongs *totally* to him, to be used in some way in divine worship. Thus a church that is consecrated—not simply blessed, as are most churches in our country—may never be used for anything else except worship. If it cannot be a church, it must be taken down. A chalice is consecrated and has only one use. Nuns may be consecrated by the ceremony in the ritual called the Consecration of Virgins. When this happens the Church is setting them aside, like a chalice, for God's exclusive use, which means, in practice, that their whole life is to be one act of worship. Now the *character* of baptism is a sign of our consecration. Yes, like the consecrated virgin, our whole life, *because of our baptism,* is to be one act of worship. Actually all the Church does to the nun is to ratify her adult acceptance of her baptismal commitment.

When the Church consecrates a person, place, or thing, it uses its most sacred oil, chrism. In fact, chrism is *the* oil of consecration. For example, when a church building is consecrated, the bishop anoints with chrism the twelve crosses that are painted on its walls, and these crosses then remain as signs of its consecration. So the three sacraments that confer the sign of personal consecration employ this sacred oil.[11]

We can see why holy orders consecrates the recipient, but why does baptism? Because it incorporates us into Christ and therefore makes us one with him whose whole life was consecrated for the use of the Father. We are back to the fact that because of baptism we operate principally by Christ as our head, as our agent of action. Confirmation, as we shall see, as the completion of baptism, is a fuller, deeper, more mature commitment to Christ's worship of the Father.

Worship for the Christian means fundamentally Christ's worship. Our way to the Father is through him, just as our way of worship is his. He is priest and offering. So our incorporation in him, whether in the sacraments of baptism, confirmation, or orders, is a progressively complete union with him as priest and offering. These three sacraments confer incorporation in Christ, consecrated priest par excellence. The *character,* then, is an interior sign of this union.

But the character is more than just a sign. Considered as a "seal," it is, as it were, a "stamping" with the image of Christ. He is, as St. Paul wrote, the Father's concrete image: "This Son is the radiant reflection of God's glory, and the express image of his nature...." And, as he himself said: "He who sees me sees the Father."[12] Baptism, confirmation, and holy orders confer the general likeness of Christ. This means that the recipient has the obligation to act as Christ, to fill in the details of the general picture. Because the character is the image of Christ it gives a title to all graces necessary for the recipient to live out this image, and is another permanent principle for reliving Christ's life. Since it is only given by sacraments, we see another important reason for the sacraments, we are better able to realize that Christian life is sacramental life.

The really astounding thing about the sacraments is that *they,* and not those who receive them, do all these things: *they* produce these effects. The sacraments, as we have seen, cause sacramental grace as Christ's instruments: when they are performed they *produce* the grace of which he is the source and, therefore, principal cause. The production of grace does not depend on the recipient, but on the application of the form to the matter.[13]

The teaching of the Church is that the sacraments give grace to those who place no obstacle in the way.[14] Looking at the matter more positively we can say that a sacrament is an encounter with God that results from his act and from the act of the recipient. We have seen what God's act is, now let us look at ours.

From all that has been said you will certainly conclude that our act is love. God's gift of grace is in reality the gift of himself, and, therefore, an act of completely unselfish love, unselfish because we are unnecessary to God's happiness. Our act, then, is a corresponding return of love. God advances to us in the sacraments and we advance to him. (We could not even make that step without the gift of his grace.)

No matter what other dispositions we bring to the sacraments, faith, hope, contrition, our act must consist fundamentally of love, choosing God as our good, desiring union with him, willing his good.

Since the general effect of the sacraments is to confer and deepen adopted sonship, after baptism our love must be filial, that of sons. Or, rather, that of the Son by nature, whose love is the Holy Spirit. The Father advances toward us as our Father, we, toward him as his sons in the Son. Reliving the life of Christ, we relive especially his interior life: his intentions, attitudes, virtues, all of which can be summed up by his sacrificial love. So when we step forward in the sacramental encounter our act is really the love of Christ going to meet his Father, with the one word, "Father!"

Since the sacraments are acts of Christ causing sonship in us, making us into himself, we go to the Father in him. We bring him ourselves, our human nature, as a new incarnation for him. Our act of love is one of donation, of belonging to him as our head, much as his human nature in one eternal act of love gives itself to his Person of Son.

The Spirit is the immediate contact of the Trinity with us, with our spirit. Hence, our first encounter in the sacraments is with him. He takes the initiative. As St. Paul says:

> ...[T]he Spirit also helps our weakness. For we do not know what we should pray for as we ought, but the Spirit himself pleads for us with unutterable sighs. And he who searches the heart knows what the Spirit desires and that he in accord with God's designs pleads for the saints.[15]

As the Father sent the Son, now both send the Spirit who forms us into Christ. Our act in the encounter is the love that is the image of himself—selflessness.

We may go to confession weekly, receive Holy Communion frequently, even daily, and we are troubled because nothing within us is changed. Our confessions are always the same, the Eucharist seems to do nothing for us. Something, then, is wrong with our part of the encounter. We are not bringing to it the fundamental disposition of that love that surrenders oneself totally to the Holy Spirit to be made into Christ. The sacraments produce the grace, but without this love the Spirit can hardly fill in the details of the image with which the sacramental characters of baptism and confirmation have "stamped" us. Without this love we resemble people who regularly draw an allowance and then die of malnutrition.

One final word on the subject: sacramental grace is influenced not only by the sacraments themselves, but also by us as individuals. It is created for us individually, "custom made." As Fr. Mersch wrote:

> Grace is personal in each man. In each individual it has traits that correspond to peculiarities of race, nation, age, contemporary civilization, temperament, and character; it has its own unique quality that makes it quite distinct, though not separate, from the grace of all other men.[16]

Let us now synthesize briefly the first nine chapters. We are on the supernatural level because the Father has re-created us in the image of the Son. The actual re-creation is the work of the Holy Spirit, and the means are the sacraments. These are the life and work of Christ made present and effective by certain symbolic actions. Thus the mysteries of Christ and the action of the Spirit form us into Christ.

Notes

1.   Jn 3:5.
2.   Jn 6:53-54.
3.   Émile Mersch, S.J., *The Theology of the Mystical Body* (St. Louis: B. Herder Book Co., 1955), p. 556.
4.   Jn 15:5.
5.   Cf. Mersch, *The Whole Christ,* p. 464.
6.   Cf. *Summa Theologiae,* III, Q. 62, a. 2.

7.   For a good example of this, see M.M. Philipon, O.P., *The Sacraments in the Christian Life* (Westminster, Md.: The Newman Press, 1954), p. 31.

8.   1 Cor 12:12.

9.   1 Cor 6:15.

10.   Cf. Paul Palmer, S.J., *Sacraments and Worship* (Westminster, Md.: The Newman Press, 1954), p. 86; *Summa Theologiae,* III, Q. 63, arts. 1 and 3.

11.   Only the bishop is consecrated with chrism. The newly ordained's hands are anointed with the oil of catechumens. The bishop receives the *fullness* of the priesthood, in which the priest participates as his auxiliary. Therefore the latter is, strictly speaking, not consecrated. See Chapter 15.

12.   Heb 1:3; Jn 14:9.

13.   Cf. *Summa Theologiae,* III, Q. 62, a. 1.

14.   For a treatment of obstacles in the sacraments, see A. Tanquerey, *A Manual of Dogmatic Theology* (New York: Desclée Company, 1959), Vol. 2, pp. 202-203.

15.   Rom 8:26-27.

16.   Mersch, *The Theology of the Mystical Body,* p. 613.

T E N

Baptism: Incorporation and Adoption

"In fact, by a single Spirit all of us, whether Jews or Greeks, slaves or free men, were introduced into the one body through baptism, and were all given to drink of a single Spirit."[1] These words of St. Paul to the Corinthians give clearly and succinctly the reasons for baptism: incorporation in Christ, and the giving of the Spirit of adoption.

Incorporation is the first effect of baptism, that is, baptism puts us into the Mystical Body, the "whole Christ," and *as a result* we are given the other effects. (Of course, all of this happens simultaneously, but we have to make distinctions as to the *logical* procedure in order to appreciate just what does happen.) We understand better the importance of baptism and its particular grace when we realize that the baptism of desire does not incorporate us into the Mystical Body. It gives sanctifying grace, but it cannot effect that union with Christ that makes the person and him one Body.[2] So our Australian bushman of Chapter 1 can reach the beatific vision *through* Christ, but not *in* him and *with* him.

"Well," you say, "what's so bad about that? Just so he can make it." I have already answered that objection when I stated that adopted sonship was much better than "sonship-in-general," and that living by Christ's life was not only immeasurably superior but also a good deal easier than living merely by our own. But another answer you can deduce from what has already been said: we are re-created by Christ in the image of the Trinity, more particularly in his own image, to be by adoption what he is by nature. This is the mystery of God's will with regard to us, this is his good pleasure.[3] We are to be *one in Christ,* to be the Son, because we are in real, physical, organic union with him, receiving from him a nature like that which he has in common with the Father. Their possession of this one nature makes them one; our possession with him of the created share of this nature makes us one. As Father and Son are one, so the Son and we, and therefore, the Father and we. "All are to be one; just as you, Father, are in me and I am in you, so they, too, are to be one in us."[4] Christian life, then, is life not only *through* Christ, but *in* and *with* him, because the Father has so decreed it. As God is Trinity, so Christian life is to be Trinitarian.

"The head and members are as one mystic person..." wrote St. Thomas.[5] It is this one mystic person that God wills—not only that we come to the beatific vision, to "save our souls," but that we come to it in and as that person. Therefore we must be baptized because—to repeat—this is baptism's first effect, this is what it does first, joins us to that person. And only baptism does this. I am not baptized in order to receive sanctifying grace and have all my sins remitted, baptism of desire can do this. Rather, I am baptized so that I can be *in* Christ, and therefore receive sanctifying grace and have all my sins remitted. This may sound rather shocking, but a little thought on the subject will show you that this is the only way we can put it if we want to demonstrate clearly the meaning of baptism. Since baptism is a sacrament, its purpose is to give grace, but according to God's purpose it confers grace only because of our physical union with Christ the head.

The second reason for baptism is to give the Spirit of adoption, the Spirit-adopting. We read in the Acts of the Apostles that while St. Peter was instructing the gentile Cornelius and his household the Holy Spirit came to them. Because of this St. Peter decided to baptize them: "Can anyone refuse the baptism of water to these people, seeing that they have received the Holy Spirit just as we did?"[6] But if they had already received the Holy Spirit why did St. Peter baptize them? It was because this visitation of the Spirit was not for the purpose of adoption: St. Peter knew that the Spirit accomplished adoption only through baptism. Later St. John would write down the mind and teaching of Christ regarding adoption by means of baptism.

Let us look at this. First, in the prologue to his Gospel, he wrote: "But to as many as welcomed him he gave the power to become children of God—those who believe in his name; who were born not of blood, or of carnal desire, or of man's will; no, they were born of God." How are we to be born of God? In Chapter 3 St. John gave us Christ's simple answer: "I am telling you the plain truth: unless a man is born of water and the Spirit, he cannot enter the kingdom of God!"[7] Christ's teaching on baptism, then, was that it is a rebirth: we are born as creatures, reborn as sons. This adoption is the work of the Spirit, who adopts only in baptism.

St. Cyril of Alexandria wrote:

> [Christ] has, therefore, brethren like himself, who bear the image of His divine nature by way of sanctification; for that is the way Christ is formed in us, inasmuch as the Holy Spirit as it were transforms us from what is human to what is His.... On those who have been made partakers of His divine nature through participation in the Holy Spirit, there is somehow stamped the suprasensuous likeness to Christ, and the beauty of the inexpressible divinity gleams in the souls of the saints.[8]

In this beautiful passage St. Cyril expresses the fact that the Spirit by adopting us as sons elevates us to the very life of the Son, which then becomes the basis for our own.

The adopting Spirit is therefore the baptizing Spirit: we are "initiated by the Spirit"... "saved through the sanctification which the Spirit effects."[9] Read the blessing of baptismal water that occurs in the Easter

Vigil for confirmation of this. For example, this passage: "...you open the fountain of baptism to all the people of the world that they may be made new, that under the rule of your majesty it might receive the grace of your only-begotten Son from the Holy Spirit." And this, which is sung three times while the priest dips the paschal candle, symbol of the risen Christ, into the water: "May the power of the Holy Spirit come down into the fullness of this fountain." Commenting on this St. Cyril of Jerusalem wrote: "...look for its [the water's] saving power by the operation of the Holy Spirit, for you cannot be initiated but by means of both the Spirit and the water.... The water washes the body and the Spirit seals the soul...."[10]

The "water and the Spirit" are nicely linked by Christ later in St. John's Gospel: "'He who believes in me will, as the Scripture has said, himself become a fountain out of which streams of living water are flowing forth.' He meant by this the Spirit whom those who believed in him were destined to receive." Here we clearly see water as a sign for the Holy Spirit, who is sent when the form is applied to it. This pronouncement also specifies what Christ meant by these words to the Samaritan woman: "No, the water which I will give him will become in him a fountain of water welling up into eternal life."[11] Christ's water is the Spirit who acts through the instrumentality of baptismal water. But he not only acts as in that instant but is given to abide with the baptized: he "wells up into eternal life." He stays to act and, like a fountain, continuously flows. At Pentecost he came to stay in the Church. When St. Peter baptized Cornelius and his household he intended to give not only the adopting Spirit but also the abiding Spirit. Hence he saw baptism also as doing for the Church what Pentecost had done for the Apostles and, therefore, as being the Church's Pentecost.[12]

The fundamental reason for the vital, dynamic role of the Holy Spirit in baptism is that we are baptized into the risen Christ, and the resurrection is the spirit's work: "...the Spirit of him who raised Jesus from the dead...."[13]

St. Paul sees baptism as union, radically, with Christ's death, but, finally, with his resurrection and with all that that implies and gives.

> Do you not know that all of us who have been baptized into union with Christ Jesus have been baptized into union with his death? Yes, we were buried in death with him by means of Baptism, in order that, just as Christ was raised from the dead by the glorious power of the Father, so we also may conduct ourselves by a new principle of life. Now since we have grown to be one with him through a death like his, we shall also be one with him by a resurrection like his.[14]

The ancient baptismal fonts were pools; for St. Paul immersion in the water was participation in Christ's death, and coming up out of it, in his resurrection.

This, of course, is symbolism; our participation in the resurrection does not derive from resemblance to

Christ's rising from the tomb but from necessity. Baptism has to be resurrection for the Christian, a physical union with this mystery. You will recall that in Chapter 5 we considered that only the *risen* Christ could give grace, because not until his human nature experienced the full effects of the divine Sonship to which it is hypostatically united could Christ give adopted sonship to our human nature. I repeat, because it belongs here, the last sentence of that section: "Christ must attain to the fulfillment of his own Sonship before he can be the source of adoption." His resurrection became the moment for conferring adoption, that which he had merited. His time of merit was over, now was the time for giving. Hence, baptism, the beginning of adoption in us, derives from Christ's resurrection, the beginning of the fullness of Sonship in him.

Two passages from St. Paul's Epistle to the Colossians beautifully express this:

> Further, he is the head of his body, the Church, in that he is the beginning, the first to rise from the dead, so that he may have preeminence over every creature. For it pleased God the Father that in him all fullness should dwell, and that through him God should reconcile to himself every being, and make peace both on earth and in heaven through the blood shed on the cross.... For in him is embodied and dwells the fullness of the Godhead.... Buried with him by Baptism, you also rose with him by your faith in the power of God who raised him from the dead.[15]

This is the fullness of which St. John wrote: "And of his fullness we have all received a share..."[16]—Sonship, his own and ours, which at his resurrection he can give for the first time as head of his Mystical Body.

In Chapter 5 we saw the relation of the Holy Spirit to the incarnation and resurrection: he accomplished these acts because he is the union and the power of God, the Spirit of holiness. Our baptism was for us incarnation as well as resurrection. The adopting Spirit, as union, power, and holiness, united our human nature to the divine-human Son, to the "whole Christ." Our "flesh" became the Word. From that instant something happened to us similar to what happened to Christ's human nature: we lost the right to be exclusively our own agent of action; the Person of Christ would henceforth be in some way one with our *person*. Incorporation in Christ means that *Christ* is to live in and through us. Incorporation for us, then, was incarnation, the act of the Spirit.

But we are incorporated not into Christ in the womb of Mary but into him as risen. This means that we, too, have risen. Hence, what the Holy Spirit did for Christ at the resurrection he did for us at baptism. But what did he do for Christ? He united his dead body to his soul. (Of course, both had to be united, even in death, to the Person of the Son. It is the separation of the human soul from the body that constitutes death.) Also, at that instant, he gave to soul and body, as I have already said, the complete effects of the divine Sonship, filling them with the fullness of the Son.

How does this relate to our baptism? One of St. Paul's great points of emphasis is that the resurrection of Christ not only means the resurrection of the baptized, but also produces, or causes, it. For example: "And if the Spirit of him who raised Jesus from the dead dwells in you, then he who raised Christ Jesus from the dead will also bring to life your mortal bodies because of his Spirit who dwells in you."[17] We are baptized into the risen Christ, therefore our bodies shall be reunited to our souls. We may not have thought of the resurrection of the body as being a direct effect of baptism, but that is St. Paul's teaching. And as the Holy Spirit did this for Christ, so will he do this for us.

But the full effects of Sonship, which he conferred on Christ's humanity, he also confers through baptism: our human nature knows what it is to be organically united to Christ. For one thing, we are able to live by our spirit, rather than by our "flesh." This means that we are able to live on the supernatural rather than on the natural level. "You, however, are not carnal [from *sarx*] but spiritual [from *pneuma*], if indeed the Spirit of God dwells in you. But if anyone does not have the Spirit of Christ, he does not belong to Christ."[18] The Spirit gives us the life of Christ to be our life, and thus he gives us the life of our spirit by which we can "put to death" a purely natural mode of existence. Just as the incarnation gave Christ's human nature the life of the Son, the Spirit by baptism gives our nature Christ's way of being Son. So we must be "led by the Spirit of God" in order to be adopted sons. His "glorification" of our humanity is accomplished practically, daily, by the infused virtues and the gifts and by actual graces, all of which make it possible for poor human nature to live Christ's life. Thus we see how we are to supernaturalize the natural, as we read in the first chapter: to let Christ take over our lives, much as the Son took over the human nature by the resurrection.

But we know that our glorification is far from complete. True, we are now able to live as Christ, a completely supernatural elevation of human nature, but "the going is rough." Besides, we must still fulfill the lawful demands of the body; we suffer and shall die. But if Christ, the Prototype, is the first to rise from the dead, then shall we. So at his second coming our resurrection grace will be complete, our glorification will be accomplished. It is consoling to realize that our weak, tired, sick bodies will at length fully participate in the grace of adopted sonship. Our baptism is a "part payment" as well as a pledge of the full reality. The Spirit will do for us what he did for Christ, because we are baptized into his resurrection. Granted that this time is one of trial, of testing our love, complete glorification now would be out of the question.

St. Paul wrote of the risen Christ: "The last Adam became a spirit imparting life."[19] The revelation of the Holy Spirit is of a Person who is God, but directed to Father and Son because he is their love. The meaning of this passage of St. Paul is that at the resurrection Christ is filled with the divine life which he can now give—*spirit* here is life, God's own life, but to be imparted outside the Trinity in a created form.

In his Second Epistle to the Corinthians St. Paul wrote:

> Now the Lord is the spirit, and where this spirit of the Lord is, there is freedom. But all of us, reflecting as in a mirror the Lord's glory, are being transformed into his very image from one degree of splendor to another, such as comes from the Lord who is the spirit.[20]

The meaning of *spirit* in this passage is the same as above, but here St. Paul is more explicit as to what Christ, considered as God-giving, gives: after the initial grace of adoption in baptism—"reflecting as in a mirror the Lord's glory"—he transforms us more and more into himself, so that, as I have said, we can be by adoption what he is by nature, so that we can be the Son to the Father. But while we get this ability to be more and more Christ from himself as the meriting source—"such as comes from the Lord who is the spirit"—we get it immediately from him who is the contact of the Trinity with man, the Holy Spirit—"Whoever are led by the Spirit of God, they are the sons of God."[21]

We can see the Holy Spirit's role in baptism, then, from his role in Christ's resurrection: he confers union and Sonship. The Spirit who has incorporated us in the risen Christ fills us with his Sonship, and, at his second coming, will reunite our bodies to our souls. He is the adopting Spirit, the Pentecostal Spirit, abiding in the Church until Christ's coming.

There are several elements in Christ's baptism by St. John that we must consider here. John's baptism had no power to give grace and remit sins; it was an action symbolic of repentance, and supposed that the man submitting to it was a sinner. When Christ asked John for baptism he explained that it was to "fulfill, as is proper for us, all just demands." What were these just demands? St. Paul gave us the answer: "For our sakes God made sin of him who knew no sin, so that in him we might become God's holiness."[22] It was fitting that Christ, who became for the purpose of atonement every sinner who ever was and would be, who took on himself every sin as if it were his own, should submit to this sign of repentance. This action—John's baptism—he would link to his death and resurrection, and by the Spirit make it into the action of adoption. The descent of the Spirit and the presence of the Trinity, joined to the water, are all the elements of Christian baptism.[23]

But Christ would later refer to his death as his baptism: "...can you drink the cup that I am to drink, and be baptized with the baptism with which I am to be baptized?"[24] His death was his baptism in that by it he merited Sonship for his human nature, that is, the full effects on it of its union with the Son. We have already seen this in Chapter 5 and so it needs no explanation here. Remember, though, that what Christ merited for us he must first merit for himself. His resurrection was his baptism in that it conferred on him the Sonship merited.

Since, then, baptism incorporates us into the risen Christ, it is the symbolic action that makes present his death and resurrection. Of course it makes present all of his acts, by which he merited for us sonship with its concomitant graces, but especially and essentially these two acts. At every baptism at which we shall henceforth assist, we must, at the actual moment of baptism, realize: now is present the personal baptism of Christ—his death and resurrection, and therefore the baptism of his child means incorporation into the risen Christ as its head, the filling of it, soul and body, with adoptive sonship. Now the death is present so that the grace it merited for this child can now be given. It is brought forward in time, to this place, to be applied to this child. Now the resurrection, too, is an actuality, because here and now actual, for this child. And by incorporation and adoption it is now dead to a life purely or primarily on the natural level. As in the risen Christ, Sonship must now dominate, for the risen life means the life of the *Son*.

Therefore the sacramental grace of baptism is relative to incorporation and adoption: it is the life of the Son. The divine life of Christ is the essential note of this sacrament, hence, of its particular grace. The Eucharist will center about his human nature, but not baptism. If I may dare say so, it causes our "hypostatic union" with Christ, not in the strict sense, but in the sense that our human nature is united to his divine nature by the instrumentality of his human acts. And because baptism puts us into the Mystical Body, it unites our person to the Person of Christ. As the Greek Fathers loved to say, it "divinizes" us. As the divine in the risen Christ completely influenced the human, so the grace of baptism is directed to the same effect, as far as this is possible, in us. To repeat: this sacramental grace makes it possible for us to live as God the Son.

The actual graces to which baptism gives us a title have for their object the actualization of this sanctifying grace: until we die they will be constantly present to enable us to put into act our sonship. The infused virtues are accordingly ordered to the domination of sonship in our daily lives. It is no easy thing, what with human nature, and weakened at that, to live out the *risen* life of Christ, which life St. Paul delineated for us:

> If, then, you have risen with Christ, seek the things that are above, where Christ is seated at the right hand of God. Set your mind on the things that are above, not on the things that are on earth. For you have died and your life is hidden with Christ in God.[25]

The virtues infused with sanctifying grace are seven powers, daily present, whereby we can supernaturalize the natural, divinize the human, let the Son of God take the direction in our lives. A mere thought of what these virtues are, and of their relation to our adopted sonship, will convince us that to live as the Son is possible. The gifts of the Holy Spirit received in baptism enable us to have the mind of the Son. They receive the Spirit's inspirations that form us into Christ by giving us his attitudes, his mentality.[26] It would hardly suffice to merely *act* as the Son, for then we would be puppets. His acts proceed from his mind.

After treating of the character of holy orders Fr. Scheeben wrote of that of baptism: "But the baptismal character enables all others, if not to reenact, at any rate to offer, this sacrifice [of the Mass] to God as their own, as a sacrifice truly belonging to them on the strength of their membership in the body of Christ."[27] The character of baptism is the first conferring of the Christian priesthood in this sense, that now as adopted sons we can offer the incarnate Son with him as *the* priest because we are in him. We truly, and not metaphorically, share in Christ's priesthood. This character, too, consecrates us to reliving the life of the Son, so that any action, which he does not direct, which is deliberately done primarily for self, will be as profane as, say, a card party held in a consecrated church. The baptismal character sets us aside for the purposes of worship.

As soon as we were baptized we were anointed with the oil of consecration, the sacred chrism. As the seal of our baptism, it was also the sign of our consecration that we had been "stamped" with the general likeness, or image, of Christ, the "final touch," as it were, of the baptismal character. But it was also related to the general priesthood of the character, because anointing with oil was the Old Testament way of consecrating the high priest. Moses first did this to Aaron, according to God's instructions.[28] Chrism is, therefore, used in holy orders, and we can see its use and purpose in baptism— the sign of priesthood.

Although the sacramental grace of baptism emphasizes the life of the Son, the divine nature in Christ, incorporation into him as head gives us a foundation, a principle, for reliving the life of the human nature. The real stimulus for this comes from the Eucharist, but the power of this later contact with Christ necessarily presupposes the basic physical union that baptism gives. We can share in Christ's life only if we are one organism with him, and baptism puts us into that organism.

So baptism is the beginning of our Christian life because it is our birth, not as ourselves, but as Christ. And as a baby grows, so does Christ grow in us, and this growth is the work of the other sacraments.

Notes

1. 1 Cor 12:13.
2. Cf. G. Van Noort, *Dogmatic Theology* (Westminster, Md.: The Newman Press, 1959), Vol. 2, p. 240. Also *Summa Theologiae,* III, Q 69, a. 5.
3. Eph 1:9-10.
4. Jn 17:21.
5. *Summa Theologiae,* III, Q. 48, a. 2.
6. Acts 10:47.
7. Jn 1:12-13; 3:5.
8. *Adversus Nestorii Blasphemias, P.G.* 76, 128–129. In Walter J. Burghardt, S.J., *The Image of God in Man According to St. Cyril of Alexandria* (Woodstock, Md.: Woodstock College, 1955), p. 112.
9. Gal 3:3; 2 Thes 2:13.
10. *Catechetical Lectures,* III, 4. In William Telfer, ed., *Library of Christian Classics* (Philadelphia: The Westminster Press, 1955), Vol. 4, p. 91. A Protestant translation.
11. Jn 7:38-39; 4:14.
12. Cf. David Stanley, S.J., "The New Testament Doctrine of Baptism," *Theological Studies,* June, 1957, pp. 207-209.

13.   Rom 8:11.
14.   Rom 6:3-5. All of Romans 6 should be read.
15.   Col 1:18-20; 2:9, 12.
16.   Jn 1:16.
17.   Rom 8:11.
18.   Rom 8:9-10.
19.   1 Cor 15:45.
20.   2 Cor 3:17-18.
21.   Rom 8:14.
22.   Mt 3:15; 2 Cor 5:21.
23.   Cf. Stanley, *loc. cit.,* p. 198.
24.   Mk 10:38. Cf. Lk 12:50.
25.   Col 3:1-3.
26.   Cf. 1 Cor 2:6-16.
27.   Matthias Joseph Scheeben, *The Mysteries of Christianity* (St. Louis: B. Herder Book Co., 1946), p. 586.
28.   Cf. Lev 8:1-12; 21:10.

ELEVEN

Confirmation: The Fullness of Sonship

Confirmation gives the fullness of the Holy Spirit, therefore the fullness of sonship. This is the essence of the sacrament, its meaning and its purpose.

It is true, we received the Holy Spirit in baptism, we "were all given to drink of a single Spirit."[1] What more is there to receive? What is this "fullness"? The reason for confirmation is that the Holy Spirit "anointed" Christ on *two* occasions: at the Incarnation, when he united the human nature to the Son; and after Christ's baptism, when he descended upon him in the form of a dove. Our baptism was our first anointing by the Spirit, our Incarnation. Because the Son received a second, so must we adopted sons. "Confirmation extends to us the mystery of the baptism of Christ in the Jordan when the Father publicly proclaimed him Son at the inauguration of his messianic mission."[2]

St. Peter referred to Christ's second anointing when addressing Cornelius and his household: "You know how God anointed him with the Holy Spirit and with power, and he went about doing good and healing all who were in the power of the devil because God was with him."[3] The Spirit had given his human nature the fullness of divine Sonship already in the womb of Mary, there is no question of this. But the Incarnation, as we have seen, existed only for the redemption, for Christ's role as the atoning Messiah, for his role as head of the Mystical Body. Son of God he certainly was in Nazareth, but eventually he must come out of retirement to act as the Messiah: to preach, break the reign of Satan, form his Apostles, suffer, die, and rise again. These strictly messianic acts were the climax of his earthly life, as they provided the motive for it.

The second anointing of Christ by the Spirit gave the fullness of Sonship to his human nature in the sense that he gave it the fullness of its mission: the power to be the instrument of the Son in the redemptive act. Christ's human nature was now perfectly fitted to be that of the Messiah. Thus the second anointing completed the purpose of the first, it completed and fulfilled the Incarnation; it, as it were, matured Christ for his life-work. We can say that it was Christ's investiture with the messianic mission. I think that there is a parallel here with the investiture of missionaries immediately before they are sent to a foreign mission. For years they have prepared themselves for this work; now at last their superior approves them, gives them an official mandate, confers the power to have authority, perform the sacraments, and preach in their new territory. They are invested with their mission.

"No sooner was Jesus baptized, than he came up out of the water, and there and then the heavens opened to his view: he saw the Spirit of God descend in the shape of a dove, and alight on him. And a voice rang out upon the air: 'This is my Son, the beloved, with whom I am well pleased.'"[4] Christ, as the first "Apostle," has offered himself for the messianic mission. The Father accepts and approves him and gives him the mandate by giving him the Spirit, who fills his human nature with messianic power. "Invested with the power of the Spirit..." St. Luke wrote of him.[5] When Christ stood up to read in the synagogue of Nazareth he unrolled the scroll of Isaiah to the passage: "The Spirit of the Lord rests upon me, because he has anointed me. He has appointed me a messenger to bring the Good News to the humble; to announce release to captives, and recovery of sight to the blind; to set the oppressed at liberty; to proclaim a year of grace ordained by the Lord." When he sat down he added: "Today the Scripture text you have just heard has been fulfilled."[6] He left Nazareth as the incarnate Son and returns as the Messiah.

So confirmation is our second anointing, with precisely the same effects as Christ's. It "...finishes the work begun by the rite of Baptism,"[7] for it carries out to completion the purpose of sonship-"messiahship": we are adopted sons only to be messiahs. Christ was not "completed" until his second anointing because he came to be the Messiah. So confirmation perfects us as sons because this sacrament is sonship realized and fulfilled. The very name indicates that the Father has given us the "seal of approval," he has by that seal confirmed the fact that we are authentic messiahs, officially invested with the messianic mission. Another meaning of *confirmation* is that this sealing with chrism confirms, officially ratifies, the profession of faith made just before the actual baptism.

Therefore we see that confirmation is not an "ornamental" sacrament, something that is proper but not exactly necessary. It is necessary if we are to be complete Christians. As such it was always given in the early Church immediately after baptism, during the Easter Vigil. The reception of the Eucharist in the Mass that followed was the third and final phase of Christian initiation. Baptism without confirmation means an imperfect initiation because something basic is missing.

What is the purpose of confirmation? This question has been answered already: to give the fullness of sonship by giving the fullness of the Spirit. Let us examine this purpose more closely. From the foregoing we should realize that it is not enough to be adopted sons. Sonship is given to us that we might be Christ in his totality, so that we might relive not only his fundamental state of Son, but also his state of Messiah, Redeemer. Therefore, baptism gave us sonship with a view to our role in the Mystical Body. Now confirmation conferred on us that role, our particular mission to the Mystical Body. Sonship in us, as in Christ, is oriented to social responsibility. While baptism is concerned more with our personal life as sons, confirmation gives us the power and mandate to carry sonship to others. God is interested in the whole body of Christ. The object of Christ's mission is to save individual men and to build his Mystical Body. In sharing in his state and mission of Redeemer we are sharing in the fulfillment of his Sonship.

But this fulfillment was given to him by the Spirit's second anointing, which bestowed on him the fullness of the Spirit. The Apostles received the Spirit of adoption on Easter, when Christ "...breathed on them and said: 'Receive the Holy Spirit.'"[8] The fullness of the Spirit, that is, the Spirit giving them the messianic mission, came to them on Pentecost. So confirmation is Pentecost for the one receiving it, for by it he receives not the adopting Spirit of Easter, but the "messianic" Spirit of Pentecost. We see this in the prayer that the bishop says at the conclusion of the ceremony: "O God, you gave your Holy Spirit to your Apostles. You willed that through them and their successors the same gift should be delivered to all the faithful."[9]

Confirmation, then, gives the Holy Spirit; it can be called baptism by the Spirit. We read in the Acts of the Apostles:

> Now when the apostles in Jerusalem heard
> that Samaria bad accepted the word of God,
> they sent Peter and John to them. On their
> arrival they prayed for the Samaritans, that
> they might receive the Holy Spirit. As yet he
> had not come on any of them, because they
> had only been baptized in the name of the

> Lord Jesus. Then Peter and John laid their
> hands on them, and they received the Holy
> Spirit.[10]

St. Luke in the Acts wrote of certain ones who had this Pentecostal Spirit as having his fullness: "...select from among you seven men of good reputation, full of the Spirit and of wisdom..." "...Stephen, a man full of faith and of the Holy Spirit...." "But Saul (also called Paul), filled with the Holy Spirit...." "But the disciples continued to be filled with joy and the Holy Spirit."[11]

After his baptism Christ was directed and impelled, as it were, by the Spirit. St. Luke, the chronicler of the Pentecostal Spirit, has indicated this more than the other evangelists: "Jesus, full of the Holy Spirit, turned away from the Jordan and was led by the Spirit into the desert to be put to the test by the devil for forty days." "Invested with the power of the Spirit, Jesus now returned to Galilee...." "Inspired by the occasion, he exulted in the Holy Spirit...." "...I drive out demons by the finger of God...."[12]

After Pentecost the Holy Spirit directed the Church, as he did Christ in his public life. The Acts abound in such expressions as: "Yet they were not able to cope with the wisdom and the Spirit by whom he [Stephen] spoke." "At the same time it [the Church] increased in numbers through the exhortation inspired by the Holy Spirit." "...the Spirit bade me to accompany them without hesitation." "As they were celebrating the liturgical worship of the Lord and fasting, the Holy Spirit said, 'Set apart immediately for me Saul and Barnabas for the work to which I have called them.'" "They passed through Phrygia and the Galatian country, because they had been forbidden by the Holy Spirit to speak the word in the province of Asia. When they came to the frontier of Mysia, they tried to enter Bithynia, but the Spirit of Jesus did not permit them."[13]

The names for confirmation in the early Church were the sacrament of the seal and the sacrament of anointing, names closely interrelated. First let us look at the latter. *Anointing* here meant the anointing with the Holy Spirit which Christ received after his baptism, because that is the inspired metaphor of the biblical writers (e.g., Is 61:1; Acts 10:38). We must understand this point; before any sacred oil was ever used the "anointing" was done by the imposition of hands. So the original meaning of the word in connection with confirmation is its relation to Christ's investiture with the fullness of the Spirit.

But there is yet a more fundamental meaning of "anointing" here. The word *messiah* is Hebrew for "the anointed one." The expected Redeemer was to be priest, king, and prophet. In the Old Testament priests and kings were consecrated for their respective missions by an anointing. Prophets were men of God consecrated either to praising God in psalms and hymns, or to carrying out specific missions from God to his people. Prophets were especially under the guidance of the "spirit of God," as we read in the accounts of Elijah, Elisha, and Ezekiel.[14] The Redeemer would be priest par excellence, the great and final King of the people of God, and Man of

God, charged with and consecrated for his divine mission. Hence he was "the anointed one," as priests and kings were anointed by oil, and prophets, by the coming upon them of the "spirit of God."

The meaning of the name *Christ* is "the anointed one"—the Greek word for Christ is *Christos,* and for anointing is *chrisma*. He is the anointed Messiah of Isaiah 61:1, the One, therefore, consecrated for the messianic mission. It was natural that the Church would confer this second anointing by the Spirit by means of the visible sign of anointing with oil, a sign that the recipient was a *Christos* in the full sense.

St. Cyril of Jerusalem brought this out in one of his catechetical lectures, around the year 348:

> Now you have been made Christ's by receiving the antitype of the Holy Spirit [anointing with chrism]; and all things have been wrought in you by imagery, because you are images of Christ. He washed in the river Jordan, and having imparted the fragrance of His Godhead to the waters, He came up from them; and the Holy Spirit in the fulness of His being lighted on Him, like resting upon like. And to you in like manner, after you had come up from the pool of the sacred streams, there was given an Unction, the antitype of that wherewith Christ was anointed; and this is the Holy Spirit....

However, for the oil itself, called, appropriately, chrism St. Cyril had the greatest veneration:

But beware of supposing that this is mere ointment. For as the bread of the Eucharist, after the invocation of the Holy Spirit, is no longer mere bread, but the body of Christ, so also this holy ointment, after the invocation, is no longer mere, or if you prefer, ordinary ointment, but the gift of Christ and of the Holy Spirit, which becomes operative through the presence of His divinity. Now this ointment is applied symbolically to your forehead and your other senses, and while your body is anointed with visible ointment, your soul is sanctified by the holy and invisible Spirit.[15]

He saw the presence of the Holy Spirit in the chrism as parallel to that of Christ in the Eucharist, a dynamic presence, waiting for the application of the outward sign to the recipient.

The essential action of confirmation now is the imposition of the bishop's hand on the head of the confirmand and the simultaneous anointing with chrism in the form of a cross. The form is: "I sign you with the sign of the cross, and I confirm you with the chrism of salvation. In the name of the Father, and of the Son, and of the Holy Spirit. Amen." Originally, as we read in the Acts, the Apostles conferred confirmation by the imposition of hands only. However, in Rome at the beginning of the third century, an anointing with consecrated oil was added after the imposition. From the fifth century on, the Western Church adopted the practice of the Eastern Church, the anointing as the essential rite. The presence of an anointing among the rites of this sacrament in the first place can be attributed to the Church's realization of the fact that confirmation is the second "anointing" of the Christian by the Holy Spirit, and that this sacrament completes his general share in Christ's priesthood. This latter concept is evident from comparisons made by St. Cyril of Jerusalem and St. Augustine of this particular anointing with the priestly anointing of Aaron.[16] Since confirmation is related to the priesthood of the laity, the Church sought for the proper sign in the Old Testament, that source of sacramental signs.

What is the particular grace of confirmation? In general we can say that it is the messianic, the public, life of Christ. If the purpose of the sacrament is to confer the fullness of sonship, then its grace has to be the power to fulfill Christ's messianic role. Sanctifying grace given by confirmation is directed to this: it parallels the divine life in Christ using his humanity as its instrument of redemption. It is the divine life in us making it possible for the Son to use our humanity in building up his Mystical Body. The actual graces of confirmation, then, urge us out of ourselves, out of our "hidden life," to be the extensions of Christ in his public life: to preach, to heal, to exorcise. They are graces for the apostolate, because this is the sacrament that gives the mandate to apostleship. Once confirmed we can never go back to Nazareth to settle down.

Confirmation completes us as Christians because it completes us as Christ. But this was in him the work of the Holy Spirit.[17] The Father fitted the human nature of Christ for his mission by the gift of the Spirit. When the Spirit, as gift of the Father, had come upon him, the strict messianic part of Christ's life began. Confirmation is the Father and Son's gift of the Spirit to us, to achieve the same effects. As Christ was, so we are to be directed by the Spirit in our life of messianic mission. This direction he gives us by means of the seven gifts.

The Spirit in the Church is dynamically present; he is here for action, our action. Hence his direction may take the form of propulsion and leading. The gifts are not his inspirations but abilities he has given us to receive these inspirations. The marvelous thing is that we have these abilities and we get these inspirations, which are the Spirit's way of directing us. Because we are confirmed we are propelled by the Pentecostal Spirit. He wants to take the lead in our lives, just as he did in those of the Old Testament prophets, the Apostles, and the public life of Christ. Our lives can be power-driven by the Spirit, if we will submit. There's the problem. Possibly, as you read this paragraph, you thought, "Certainly I'm not being propelled by the Pentecostal Spirit. I wish I were."

St. Matthew wrote: "And owing to their unbelief he did not work many miracles there."[18] Perhaps nothing very pentecostal is happening in our lives because there's really not much living faith. Perhaps too much natural level, or not enough love of God and neighbor. We have to submit to the Spirit if things are going to happen. His inspirations have come in the past and we turned them down. Now they may not come anymore. Not only must we submit to them and live by them—yes, actually live by them—but believe, hope, and pray that these words of

Christ will be realized in us: "I tell you the truth: he who believes in me will himself do the things I am doing; in fact, he will do even greater things than I do, now that I am going home to the Father...."[19]

The gifts were given us in baptism for our formation as adopted sons—the accent was on sonship and the divine nature. In confirmation they are socially ordered to our part in Christ's public life. This is not to say that the inspirations that come by way of our confirmation grace do not aim also at sanctifying us. As love of God flows over into acts of love and zeal for our neighbor, so also these latter acts make our love of God more solid and authentic. The apostolate is not the "heresy of good works."

From time to time it would be good to think of the gifts not as seven but as one, and that one the gift that is the Holy Spirit himself. For some this may be more practical to do so habitually. For really this is the great confirmation grace, isn't it: the gift of the Spirit, who confers on us the fullness of sonship, of Christ's life? As this gift he abides in us because he abides in the Church, as pentecostal presence, directing us as he directed the Apostles.

Since the sacramental grace of confirmation unites us to Christ as messiah—priest, king, and prophet—it makes of us thereby *as individuals* witnesses to Christ. Before the Ascension he told the Apostles: "...but you shall receive power when the Holy Spirit comes upon you, and you shall be my witnesses in Jerusalem and in all Judea and Samaria and even to the very ends of the earth." Later Peter and the other Apostles said to the high priest: "And we are witnesses of these events [Christ's death and resurrection], and so is the Holy Spirit, whom God has given to all who obey him."[20] The Greek word for "witnesses" in each of these passages is *martyres:* a martyr is a witness to Christ unto death. But *martyres* here does not mean "martyrs." The term simply means that "...what we have heard, what we have seen with our own eyes, what we have gazed upon, and what we have embraced with our own hands" by faith has changed our lives, and we are what we are now because Christ is real.[21] Our Christian lives testify to the fact of Christ.

The sacramental character of confirmation fills out the general outline given us by baptism in that the purpose of the sacrament is to fill out the life of Christ in us. It delineates upon us the public life, giving us a right to expect from the Spirit his own formation of us into the messiah, the anointed one. But the messiah is basically the high priest, hence the character completes the priesthood of the laity. As confirmation is the completion of baptism, it is the finalizing of the baptismal seal, the final consecration. It is the sign that this person is forever the fullness of Christ.

When we live by the Spirit of confirmation, faithful to the daily inspirations of his gifts, we live by our spirit. The Holy Spirit takes us over, makes it easy to supernaturalize the natural, to live as Christ. And having come to us as our own personal Pentecost, he sends us out in the world to witness to the validity of the life of adopted sonship.

Notes

1. 1 Cor 12:13.
2. Boniface Luykx, O. Praem., "Theology of Confirmation," *Theology Digest,* Summer, 1963, p. 81.
3. Acts 10:38.
4. Mt 3:16-17.
5. Lk 4:14.
6. Lk 4:18-19, 21.
7. A.M. Roguet, O.P., *The Sacraments: Signs of Life* (London: Blackfriars, 1954), p. 65.
8. Jn 21:22; cf. Walter J. Burghardt, S.J., *The Image of God in Man According to St. Cyril of Alexandria* (Woodstock, Md.: Woodstock College, 1955), pp. 116-117.
9. *St. Andrew Bible Missal* (Bruges: Biblica, 1962), p. 890.
10. Cf. Acts 1:5; 8:14-17.
11. Acts 6:3, 5; 13:9, 52. Cf. Acts 4:8, 31.
12. Lk 4:1-2, 14; 10:21; 11:20.
13. Acts 6:10; 9:31; 11:12; 13:2; 16:6-7. Cf. also Acts 10:19; 11:28; 13:4; 15:28; 20:22-23, 28; 21:4, 11.
14. 2 Kgs 2:9, 15-16; Ez 2:2; 3:24.
15. *Mystagogical Lectures,* III, "On Chrism," in Schaff and Wace, eds., *Nicene and Post-Nicene Fathers* (New York: The Christian Literature Company, 1894), Vol. 7, p. 149. I have modernized several words and changed "imitation" to "imagery," based on the original Greek.
16. *Ibid.,* in Palmer, p. 15.
17. Cf. Acts 8:15-17; Palmer, *op. cit.,* pp. 8, 15-16, 86. Also Pierre-Thomas Camelot, O.P., "Towards a Theology of Confirmation," *Theology Digest,* 1959, p. 68.
18. Mt 13:58.
19. Jn 14:12.
20. Acts 1:8; 5:32.
21. 1 Jn 1:1.

TWELVE

The Eucharist: The Sacrifice of Sons

The only way we can approach the Eucharist is through the covenant of the Old Testament and its sacrifices. At the moment of the first consecration Christ referred to "my covenant blood," and to "the new covenant sealed by my blood."[1] His way of procedure here, separating the blood from the body, followed that of the temple sacrifices. Then, too, the covenant meant God's people; their sacrifices ratified and expressed their particular relationship with him. Christ's covenant blood would lead these people to their ultimate destiny—his Mystical Body, sons in the Son. Thus to see the Eucharist as sacrifice and sacrament or, rather, as sacramental sacrifice we must first see it in its covenant setting.

The covenant, which God made originally with Abraham, he renewed with his sons and principally with Moses and the Israelites during the exodus. Its first effect was to set up a most personal relationship between

God and the Jews. He began the Ten Commandments, for example, with "I, the Lord, am *your* God," and always Moses referred to him in relation to the Jews as "the Lord, your God."[2] The intimacy that existed between the Jews and God, his tenderness and care for them, can be seen in Moses' recounting God's favors to them during the exodus. These words, for example, are an apostrophe of wonder at the bond which the covenant created: "Ask now of the days of old, before your time, ever since God created man upon the earth; ask from one end of the sky to the other: Did anything so great ever happen before? Was it ever heard of? Did a people ever hear the voice of God speaking from the midst of fire, as you did, and live? Or did any god venture to go and take a nation for himself from the midst of another nation?..."[3] The Jews were truly God's special people, his particular possession.

Two facts stand out in this covenant: the bond that existed between God and his people, and the union of their wills with his. "Be careful, therefore, to do as the Lord, your God, has commanded you, not turning aside to the right or to the left, but following exactly the way prescribed for you by the Lord, your God...." Because the Jews were God's people they had an obligation to behave as such, it is true, and their attitude can be summed up as one of reverential fear: "I will have them hear my words, that they may learn to fear me as long as they live in the land and may so teach their children." But the basic and essential attitude that God wished for them was one of love—the people of God responding to his love for them. "Hear, O Israel! The Lord is our God, the Lord alone! Therefore, you shall love the Lord, your God, with all your heart, and with all your soul, and with all your strength." Circumcision was the sign of the covenant, an external sign that Moses did not hesitate to interpret as a reminder of this interior response to God: "Circumcise your hearts...."[4]

Sacrifice ratified the covenant that God and his people made on Mount Sinai. When Moses came down from the mountain and the people had assured him of their part of the covenant—"We will do everything that the Lord has told us"—he ordered a sacrifice. The blood of the animals he divided: half he splashed on the altar, the other half he sprinkled on the people.[5] This act sealed the covenant because it expressed it on both sides: God giving himself to his people, they giving themselves to him, and the bond—expressed by the blood—that now existed between him and them, and between the individual Jews, a blood relationship. What better sign of union could there be than that of blood?

The only explanation of the Old Testament sacrifices is the fact of the covenant. These were all covenant sacrifices, in that they comprised the worship of God by his own especially loved people. Thus they were the great means of preserving the covenant attitude among the Jews: reverential fear and loving intimacy, and, therefore, fidelity to the will of their God. We can say that the sacrifices were the official means of binding God and his people together and of forming them into a holy people. We must note, too, that only the covenant people were able to offer these sacrifices.

Leviticus lists and prescribes for the various kinds of sacrifice. There is the holocaust, the sacrifice in which the whole animal, except the hide, was burned. Peace offerings were in reality sacrificial meals in which part of the sacrificed animal was eaten by all participating. Sin-offerings won God's forgiveness for sins of inadvertence, although not for those of malice.[6] While we do not think of it as such because it was a domestic rite, the Passover supper was also a sacrifice: "This is the Passover sacrifice of the Lord."[7] It was an atonement sacrifice, a sin-offering, by which the Jews were spared from God's wrath by means of the paschal lamb's blood. This is most important for our study of the Eucharist, for the sacrament, as we know, was instituted at the Passover sacrifice.

One essential feature of Old Testament sacrifice must be emphasized: the separation of the animal's blood from its body. This blood had to be either splashed on the sides of the altar or poured out at the altar's base. The reason for this was that the Jews considered blood as the seat of life, particularly of the soul, the *nephesh* (cf. Chapter 2). "But make sure that you do not partake of the blood; for blood is life, and you shall not consume this seat of life with the flesh." As such, then, blood belonged especially to God, and, poured out on the altar, it was able to symbolize that the offerer freely gave his life to its rightful owner. Leviticus gives another meaning of this gesture: "Since the life of a living body is in its blood, I have made you put it on the altar, so that atonement may thereby be made for your own lives, because it is the blood, as the seat of life, that makes atonement."[8] The life of the victim satisfied God, who, in justice, could take the life of the guilty offerer.

Another important element was the sacrificial meal. Two types of sacrifice, the peace-offering and the Passover supper, were definitely such meals.

> The main characteristic of a peace-offering...
> was the sacrificial banquet at which Yahweh
> was host and the immolator was guest at the
> "Lord's table." Yahweh returned part of the
> sacrificed animal to the individual who had
> offered it, a sign of the bond of peace and
> friendship that had arisen between them.[9]

Fr. Cooke recently wrote of this:

> ...there is the aspect of communion with
> Yahweh that is especially noticeable in the
> "peace offerings"...for in these sacrifices
> there was the idea of a meal shared with God;
> there is the pledge of one's friendship and
> devotion to Yahweh signified by the offering of
> a gift.[10]

The sacrificial meal was a perfect expression of the covenant: the offerer responded to God's gift of himself by a gift which symbolized his own self; the meal was both sign and means of that bond of unity and union of wills that the covenant stood for.

We are now able to understand the Eucharist as the meal-sacrifice of the covenant people. Christ brought the covenant to its fulfillment in every way: he united the people of God to his own Person by means of the human nature he had in common with them; he was victim and priest of the one sacrifice to which the others led; he left this sacrifice to his people to be sacramentally re-presented, and left it as a meal-sacrifice for the sake of unity.

Let us see all this in the light of the words of consecration. First of all, it is evident that Christ was establishing a new covenant in place of the old: "This chalice is the new covenant sealed with my blood."[11] In the accounts of Matthew and Mark he referred to his "covenant blood." The covenant on Sinai was ratified by blood, which Moses both poured out on the altar and sprinkled on the people. Christ's covenant would be ratified also by the separation of his blood from his sacrificed body, and this blood, he said, would be shed, or poured out, for many. The draining of his blood on Calvary paralleled Moses' rite that sealed the covenant, as well as the pouring out of the victims' blood on the altar in subsequent sacrifices. When Christ anticipated this sacrificial act at the Last Supper, he was doing something that his observers could understand: he was indeed establishing a new covenant because he was ratifying it in the accepted way, by a covenant-sacrifice, by the separation of blood which would be poured out.[12]

This fact of the new covenant is the very foundation of Christianity, just as that of the old was the foundation of all of the mutual relations between God and his people. Fr. Cooke writes: "...for the idea that one has of the redemption, of grace, of the Church, of a sacramental system, will necessarily be conditioned by the meaning one attaches to Christ's new covenant."[13] The old covenant meant a special bond between God and the Jews. He could even speak of them thus: "Israel is my son, my first-born. Hence I tell you: Let my son go, that he may serve me." The new covenant means something similar and yet entirely different: there is only one first-born, and that is Christ. Those who are born after him are born into him, so that they and he make up the whole Christ, sons in the Son: "...for those whom he has fore-known, he has also predestined to be conformed to the image of his Son, so that this Son should be the first-born among many brothers."[14] What was metaphor under the terms of the old covenant becomes reality under those of the new. People of God become sons of God because of the sacrifice of the Son.

But the covenant-sacrifice was at the same time atonement sacrifice: "...for this is my covenant-blood, which is about to be shed for the sake of many, with a view to forgiveness of sins."[15] The purpose of the new covenant is the bond of sonship; its condition is the atonement by the Messiah. The blood that ratifies this covenant also removes that which would prevent the intimacy between the Father and his adopted sons. The firstborn assumes the guilt and makes the atonement. As sin-offering for all his blood is poured out at the base of the altar.

There are two essential points about which we must be clear at this stage. First, the actual covenant was made on the cross on Good Friday. Christ's death was its condition as well as its ratification. Second, while all covenant-sacrifices were renewals of the covenant, they were at base worship. But the worship that they expressed was not just that of man adoring God, but that of God's people adoring their God. It was something far more personal and loving. The one sacrifice of the new covenant expresses the worship of the Son-made-man, particularly through his obedience to the Father's will. Here his love of the Father impels him to offer, not a symbolic victim, but his own human life. His sacrifice is not only for, but also as the human race, therefore his act of supreme worship, being that of the firstborn, was made in the name of us all, he worshiped for us.

What Christ did at the Last Supper was to anticipate his sacrifice of the next day by giving the Apostles the separation of his blood from his body under the signs of bread and wine. Why anticipate? "Do this as my memorial," he said, and, "Do this, as often as you drink it, in remembrance of me."[16] He wished to give his own sacrifice to his sons to be their sacrifice until his second coming, the very same sacrifice, but henceforth to be made present by means of the signs he designated. In other words, Christ was giving to the Church his death to be made present sacramentally.

This sacramental presence is the Eucharist; therefore the Eucharist is essentially the Mass. We tend to divide the Eucharist into sacrifice and sacrament, but such a division must not be erected into a rigid dichotomy. In reality it is Christ's sacrifice made present on the altar in a sacramental way. Communion, as a sacrificial meal, belongs therefore to the sacrifice. The Hosts reserved in the tabernacle actually belong to the Mass: they have been consecrated at one Mass and are given as part of the sacrificial meal in another. Even when Communion is given outside of Mass it is the meal of the sacrifice.

The Mass is a sacrament because it is the re-presentation of Christ's death by means of signs. The idea of a sacrament is that the sign must signify the reality that it is a symbolic action, which relates to an action of Christ. Now the signs that Christ used at the Last Supper were bread and wine, and the symbolic action he performed was changing these into his body and blood. What do these two signs signify? There can be only one reality—his death. We must note well that Christ did not say, "This is my human nature," but, "This is my body, this is my blood." When the bread and wine are changed into his body and blood, what is missing? His human soul. The only thing that the words of consecration do is to make present Christ's body and blood. And since the soul is not *thereby* made present, it is Christ as dead who is represented.

Christ's body and blood in the Mass are not those of the suffering Christ, as he was before or at the moment of his death, but of the glorified Christ, seated at the right hand of the Father. Actually, now he is not dead, but very much alive. Hence, although all the consecration of the Mass does and is concerned with doing is to make present on the altar only Christ's body and blood, as a fact his whole body is present in his blood and his blood in his body, and his soul is present, too, vitalizing the whole. As a fact, I say, because since Christ is living, the complete Christ "comes along," too, to join the two sacramental elements. But, as I said above, all the sacrament does is change bread and wine into the body and blood. The rest, as it were, accompany them.[17] If an Apostle were to have consecrated bread and wine while Christ was actually dead, the body and blood would have been in every way separated and the soul would not have been present, because that would have been Christ's condition at the time.[18]

The sacrament of the Eucharist is accomplished by the consecration, for at that moment the reality that the signs signify is, by the words that give them meaning, present under their symbolism. But what about the grace element? Is not the purpose of a sacrament to give grace? Remember, the Eucharist is the sacrifice of Christ in sacramental form, hence, what it achieves is first and essentially the presence of that sacrifice. It is the one and only sacrifice of the new covenant whereby we are sons, and express that sonship. On God's part it is giving and acceptance—giving the grace of sonship and accepting our gift of ourselves; on our part, therefore, it is also giving and acceptance. If the purpose of Christ's death was the conferring of sonship, the result of its sacramental presence is to increase that bond. When we leave Mass we are like the people of God leaving the Temple after having offered a sacrifice—not only aware that we are covenant people but also better able to be such. St. Thomas has expressed this succinctly:

> ...[B]y this sacrament, we are made partak-
> ers of the fruit of our Lord's Passion. Hence in
> one of the Sunday Secrets (Ninth Sunday
> after Pentecost) we say: *Whenever the com-*
> *memoration of this sacrifice is celebrated, the*
> *work of our redemption is enacted.*[19]

As priest and victim in the Mass Christ offers his death
there re-presented to the Father that he might give those
who participate an increase of sanctifying grace, the
virtues and gifts, and the actual graces necessary for us
to live as his new covenant people.

Christ's sacrifice was his supreme act of worship
as man of the Father. Therefore the Mass is the presence
of this worship. The very fact of the body and blood sacramentally separated on the altar *is* the worship of Christ,
because it re-presents his death. The intentions that
were in his human soul prompting this sacrifice, glory to
the Father and redemption of man, are still in him now,
prompting its re-presentation.

At the Last Supper Christ gave the Church his
supreme act of worship to be its own. As the head of his
Mystical Body it is he who, after the consecration, is
priest and victim of the sacrifice. Because of their baptismal character, his members are able to exercise their
own priesthood in the Mass by uniting themselves to
their head, in whom they truly are. Thus he and they
offer and are offered. And thus, offering the Mass in
this way, especially as co-victims of worship of the
Father, they participate in the fruits of the redemption.

The Mass is the sacrament that fulfills man's need to worship.

> The highest need of man, if we understand man's needs in their true unchangeable nature—that of offering up to God a perfect thing in sacrifice—finds its satisfaction and realization in a sacrament, as all his other needs are provided for by other sacraments.... Would it not endanger the whole of our spiritual estate if in the supernatural life we were only recipients and nothing else; if the sacramental order were nothing but a divine, unceasing enrichment of man, might it not be in danger of sliding away from God, as even heavenly spirits have turned away? But now indeed the center of the sacramental order is something active, tending towards God, for God's own sake: it is the sacrifice unto God of a most sweet odour.[20]

The Mass, then, is the sacrifice of the adopted sons, by which they express their worship that is both profoundly reverential as well as filial, because their dispositions are those of Christ.

But this sacrifice is clearly a meal-sacrifice. Christ, in instituting it, said, "Take! Eat!... Drink of it, every one of you...."[21] Those participating in the Mass are expected to share in the meal because such was the intention of Christ. The Mass is a real covenant-sacrifice in which the offerers eat the victim in order to ratify not only the sacrifice but also the covenant. The meal aspect of Mass is the same as that of, say, the peace-offerings of the former covenant. We can view Communion only in this particular setting, for this was the meaning that Christ gave it.

In the sacrificial meal of the old covenant God was the host, and the offerer, his guest. It was an aftermath of the sacrifice in that by this gesture God expressed his acceptance of the victim and therefore his unity with the offerer, and the latter, his unity with God. It was an act of mutual friendship, conditioned by the sacrifice. Thus it served to "clinch" the sacrifice and the covenant from which it sprang. "Do not those that eat the victims unite themselves with the altar?"[22] There can be no other explanation of Communion. It is the sacrificial meal *par excellence* in that this new covenant and its sacrifice are the culmination of the former.

We have considered the grace that the sacrifice in itself gives as sharing in the fruits of the redemption. What of the grace which eating the sacrificial meal gives? Christ has indicated what this grace is in a beautiful passage in John 6:

> What I tell you is the plain truth: unless you eat the flesh of the Son of Man and drink his blood, you have no life in you. He who eats my flesh and drinks my blood is in possession of eternal life; and I will raise him from the dead on the last day; for my flesh is real food, and my blood is real drink. He who eats my flesh and drinks my blood is united with me, and I am united with him. As the living Father has appointed me his ambassador, and I live because of the Father, so, too, he who eats me

> will have life because of me. This is the bread
> that has come down from heaven. It is not
> what your fathers ate; they ate and died. He
> who eats this bread will live forever.[23]

The grace is life and union. Of the latter, St. Paul wrote:

> Does not the chalice of blessings which we
> bless bring us into union with Christ through
> his blood, and does not the bread which we
> break bring us into union with Christ through
> his body? Because the bread is one, we, the
> many who all partake of that one bread, form
> one body.[24]

Commenting on this last sentence, St. John Chrysostom wrote:

> We are that very body. For what is the bread?
> The Body of Christ. What do they become who
> receive? The body of Christ; not many bodies,
> but one body. For just as bread which is made
> up of many grains is so made one that the
> individual grains nowhere appear—but are
> yet present, even though their distinction is
> not apparent because of their union—so we
> too are mutually united with one another and
> with Christ. For one is not fed on one body
> and another on another; rather, are we all
> nourished by one and the same body.[25]

The grace of the Eucharist is first of all a deepening of the union with Christ the head that originated in our baptism. "He who eats my flesh and drinks my blood is united with me, and I am united with him."

"Membership with Christ, the whole Mystical Body of Christ, ought to be considered the specific Eucharistic grace, as distinguished from all other graces."[26]

In Chapter 4 I mentioned that St. Cyril of Alexandria taught that sonship was conferred on us through two sacraments, baptism and Eucharist, that through the former we were given the Spirit of adoption and through the latter we are able to participate in Christ's human nature. Let us listen to him directly: "There was need, then, that He be in us through the Holy Spirit after a divine manner, and be mingled, so to speak, with our bodies through His sacred flesh and His precious blood, which we also have through the life-giving blessing as though in bread and wine." In the same passage he writes that Christ transforms bread and wine "...into the power of His own flesh, that we may have and partake of them as a means of life, and that the body of life may become in us a life-giving seed."[27]

I would like to cite St. Cyril of Jerusalem and, again, St. John Chrysostom on this important point. St. Cyril wrote:

> Therefore with full assurance let us partake of the body and blood of Christ. For in the figure of bread you are given His body, and in the figure of wine His blood, that when you partake of the body and blood of Christ, you become one body with Him and one blood with Him. For thus do we become Christ-bearers, since His body and blood are diffused through our members. Thus, according to

> Blessed Peter, do we become "sharers in the
> divine nature" (2 Pt 1:4).

St. Cyril's thought in this last sentence is that Christ
gives us sanctifying grace in the Eucharist through our
physical union with his human nature, which has merited grace for us. St. John Chrysostom was commenting
on Ephesians 5:30:

> Now that we might become such [one body
> with Christ], not only by way of love but also
> in very reality, we are commingled with that
> flesh. For through the food that He has given,
> this is brought about, that He may show us
> how great is His love for us.[28]

These texts make it quite clear that Eucharistic communion causes a union of our human nature with
Christ's that is to be something real and physical.
Communion is a union of body with body, soul with
soul, as well as with his divine nature.

It gives us the whole life of Christ, as it was on
earth and as it actually is now in heaven. The biblical
scholar Père Benoit had said it well:

> In the Eucharist, the central sacrament, it is
> not such or such an action of the body of
> Christ which has an effect upon us, but the
> body itself in its plenitude as the source of
> grace, which comes into us; it is not through a
> more or less superficial and ephemeral con-
> tact, but through the most intimate and lasting
> way there can be in this life: the assimilation
> of food.[29]

We have thus a real basis for acting as Christ, considered as the Son-made-man, for being sons as Christ was and is Son. We have a daily, or, at least, frequent means of reliving and continuing Christ's earthly life, because in this sacrament he gives it to us, still present in him in his interior dispositions and merit.

This physical union with Christ our head also means a union with the whole Church. This is quite clear in the light of the above texts, and hardly needs any further elaboration. If we are aware of the specific grace of eucharistic communion, which is union with Christ as head, we will know for certain that that very unity implies and supposes a union with all the other members of his body. Therefore this is the great sacrament of charity.

I have not emphasized the sanctifying grace which eucharistic communion gives because we can better see its particular nature after having considered the union with Christ's humanity which the Eucharist effects. Sacramental grace is essentially sanctifying grace, and so it is in the Eucharist. But it is given *through* our physical contact with Christ's human nature. This is especially fitting when we realize that it was this very human nature that provided the Son with an instrument of meriting grace.

This Eucharistic contact Christ gives us as a real basis for reliving his life. He has given us others—union with him in the Mystical Body, and the sacramental characters of baptism and confirmation, which impressed his likeness upon us. The mingling of his human nature with ours in Eucharistic communion allows us to fill in the details of the general likeness of the two characters. So the sanctifying grace that he gives us through Eucharistic contact is directed to this process—reliving the earthly life of our head, letting him take the initiative in all our actions. Christ lives by the Father, as he has said in John 6. That is, the divine nature, which he has as Son, the Father gives him. He who eats Christ's sacrificial meal will share in the divine nature that is in him as Son; each communicant will have within himself a principle of life similar to that which impelled Christ to do all for the Father's glory and man's sonship. In other words, he will have the underlying principle, the basis, for Christ's human acts.

So the Eucharist achieves Christ's purpose of covenant-sacrifice. It daily ratifies and maintains the covenant of Father and Son. The sacrificial meal gives the participants not only a perfect way of expressing their side of the covenant, but also the most effective means for them to accomplish its purpose—to live as the Son.

Notes

1.   Mt 26:28; Mk 14:24; Lk 22:20; 1 Cor 11:25.
2.   Cf. Dt, Chapters 5–30.
3.   Dt 4:32-34.
4.   Dt 5:32-33; 4:10; 6:4-5; 10:16.
5.   Ex 24:3-8.
6.   Cf. Lev, Chapters 1–7.
7.   Ex 12:27.
8.   Dt 12:23; Lev 17:11.

9.   Paul Heinisch, *Theology of the Old Testament* (Collegeville, Minn.: The Liturgical Press, 1955), p. 224. The reference is to Psalm 23:5.

10.   Bernard Cooke, S.J., "Synoptic Presentation of the Eucharist as Covenant Sacrifice," *Theological Studies,* March, 1960, p. 9. Cf. Lev 7:11-20; Dt 12:27.

11.   1 Cor 11:25; cf. Lk 22:20.

12.   Cf. P. Benoit, O.P., "The Holy Eucharist," *Scripture,* October, 1956, pp. 103-104. Also Cooke, *loc. cit.,* p. 29.

13.   Cooke, *loc. cit.,* pp. 29-30.

14.   Ex 4:22; Rom 8:29.

15.   Mt 26:28.

16.   Lk 22:19; 1 Cor 11:25.

17.   Cf. Anscar Vonier, O.S.B., A *Key to the Doctrine of the Eucharist* (Westminster, Md.: The Newman Press, n.d.), pp. 281-287, 329-337.

18.   Cf. *Summa Theologiae,* III, Q. 81, a. 4.

19.   *Ibid.,* III, Q. 83, a. 1.

20.   Vonier, *op. cit.,* p. 339.

21.   Mt 26:27-28.

22.   1 Cor 10:18.

23.   Jn 6:53-58.

24.   1 Cor 10:16-17.25. In Paul Palmer, S.J., *Sacraments and Worship* (Westminster, Md.: The Newman Press, 1954), p. 146.

26.   Vonier, p. 353.

27.   In Palmer, *op. cit.,* p. 140.

28.   *Ibid.,* pp. 16-17, 145.

29.   P. Benoit, O.P., "The Holy Eucharist," *Scripture,* January, 1957, p. 8.

THIRTEEN

Penance: The Destruction of Sin

Baptism, confirmation, and the Eucharist are the sacraments of initiation. In the early Church the cate-chumen received all three during the Easter vigil service; these were the sacraments that made him a Christian, which fact was emphasized by their being conferred during the same night. Now, although we receive them at intervals of years, and our transformation is gradual, they still—all three together—remain the initiation rites, the way by which Christ and the Church bring the person into Christ's life, into the fullness of sonship. Once he has received all three, he is equipped to live as the Son.

Christ has left the Church two other sacraments, however, to deal with contingencies, what I might call occasional sacraments. Because of the sin of Adam there are present in the human race two "by-products," sin and sickness. Both result from Adam's loss of gifts that God had originally given him: sin from the loss of integrity, sickness from the loss of perfect health. Integrity meant that Adam's intellect and will kept the passions and all bodily appetites easily and well under control, being perfectly docile to God's will. This was the right order for man—God ruling intellect and will, which, in turn, ruled the body. Thus man was perfectly fulfilled as a human being. The loss of integrity meant that as a human being he "fell apart." So often the body ruled the will, the intellect descended to rationalizing or downright conniving with untruth, and all were in opposition to God. As we learned in catechism, the intellect was darkened and the will weakened.

Such has been the history of man, and our own. In fact, we can say that in one-way history is the chronicle of sin. The Old Testament is the story of the sin of the people of God, longing for sin's destruction by the Messiah. We see there the consciousness of sin, of guilt, and of helplessness, yet the hope: "All we like sheep have gone astray, every one has turned aside into his own way: and the Lord has laid on him [the Messiah] the iniquity of us all."[1] Christ destroyed sin by his death, and in his resurrection he is the personification of his victory. His destruction and victory come to us by baptism. But what of the sins committed after baptism? Ideally there shouldn't be any, and the early Church was very strict on this point. But to provide for the contingency Christ established the sacrament of the second baptism, that of penance, whose purpose is to apply to us again Christ's destruction of sin.

It would be very interesting to make a study of the biblical concept of sin, tracing its development, turning over the various Hebrew and Greek words that express it, but space forbids such a project. However, because sin is a dominant theme in St. John's first Epistle, let us attempt a sketch of his theology of sin as given there, drawing also upon similar material in his Gospel.

St. John equates Christ with light: "In him was life, and the life was the light of men." "I am the light of the world. He who follows me will not walk in the dark, but have the light of life." The opposite of light is darkness, which to St. John symbolizes the very opposite of Christ: "The light shines in the darkness, and the darkness did not lay hold of it." "And this is how the sentence of condemnation is passed: the light has come into the world, but men loved the darkness more than the light, because their lives were bad." Because darkness is the absence of light, its meaning here is the absence of Christ. St. John can thus equate it with sin: "God is light, and in him there is not the faintest shadow of darkness. If we should say that we are united with him while we continue to shape our conduct in an atmosphere of darkness, we are liars; we fail to live up to the truth."[2] Sin can only exist in an atmosphere where God is not, for of its essence sin is the absence of God, and of his revelation to man, Jesus Christ.

In the last passage quoted we see another theme that was very important to St. John, that Christ is the truth. "You, however, have been anointed by the Holy

One [the Spirit], as you all know. I write to you, not because you do not know the truth, but because you do know the truth. You know, too, that a lie never springs from the truth. Who is a liar, but he who denies that Jesus is the Christ?" "...the Father's only-begotten Son—full of grace and truth!" "For this purpose I was born, and for this purpose I came into the world—to give testimony to the truth. Only he who is open to the truth gives ear to my voice." Truth is opposed by a lie, and sin is a lie because it is the absence of the truth, Christ. "He who says, 'I know him,' but does not keep his commandments, is a liar, and the truth does not dwell in him."[3]

By St. John's use of opposites we see what sin basically is—the opposite of Christ. Christ cannot coexist with sin. "You know that he made himself manifest to take away our sins—he who himself is free from sin. No one who abides in him sins; no one who sins has either appreciated or understood him.... The Son of God made his appearance for the purpose of destroying sin, the work of the devil."[4] In the garden of Gethsemane Christ came face to face with the sin of the world and what must have been for him the greatest torture of all—that in the imminent atonement be would personally take on himself all sin. "But it takes the horror of Jesus, in agony before the chalice which awaits Him, to reveal what the Old Testament used to call, in an expression which had become hackneyed, that 'which the Lord detests.'"[5]

The Lord detests sin because it is contrary to his holiness. "Everyone who cherishes this hope in God strives to be holy, just as he is holy. Everyone who commits sin commits also an act of lawlessness. That is precisely what sin is." We are now at the heart of the matter. The reason why sin and God are at extreme opposites is that sin is the one thing that God can't do, namely, choose an object other than himself. "Lawlessness" is a translation of the Greek word *anomia,* which in its biblical use means disobedience against God. What do we do when we disobey? We reject God's will and choose our own, and, in effect, we reject him to choose self. This is what we do when we sin, and this is what God can't do. He must always will himself, because God alone is unbounded perfection. Even when he loves his creation he loves it as participating in a limited way in his perfection. The divine nature alone is worthy of God, all else is related to him. Sin breaks this relation; it sees an object in a false position, as divorced from God, which is contrary to the truth. St. John used another Greek word for sin, *adikia,* here translated "act of evil"—"Every act of evil is sin...." St. Paul by means of the same word (translated as "wickedness"), expressed the opposition of sin to the truth of God: "The wrath of God is being revealed from heaven against all ungodliness and wickedness of those men who in wickedness stifle the truth of God."[6]

The Christian's relationship to God is that of an adopted child. St. John tells us in the prologue to his Gospel that we are born of God. Our activity, proceeding as it does from our share in God's nature, is that of sons: "Since you know that he is holy, you are also well aware that everyone who lives a holy life is a child of God [the Greek is "born of him"]. See what kind of love the Father has bestowed on us that we should be children not merely in name but in reality." A similarity of nature produces a similarity of life. Thus sin is entirely contrary to a child of God.

> No one who is a child of God sins, because the life-germ implanted by God abides in him, and so, he cannot sin. He is a child of God. Here is the sign which reveals who are God's children and who are the devil's: Whoever fails to lead a holy life is no child of God, neither is he who fails to love his brother." "We know that no child of God commits sin. On the contrary, the child of God guards himself, and so the evil one does not touch him.[7]

What is repugnant to God should be repugnant to his children, who, like him, are occupied in choosing him.

There is a theme of St. John that through the centuries has sounded like a trumpet blast—God is love! In this Epistle he contrasts sin with sonship and love in a way that leaves us in no doubt. "Beloved, let us love one another, because love takes its origin in God, and everyone that loves is a child of God and knows God. He who has no love does not know God, because God is love." Failure to love is sin: "But he who hates his brother is in darkness and walks in it." "He who does not love abides in death. Everyone who hates his brother is a murderer, and you know that no murderer has eternal life abiding in him." Failure to love is contrary to adopted sonship, for we are refusing to love our true brothers: "We know what love is from the fact that Jesus Christ laid down his life for us. We, too, ought to lay down our lives for our brothers. How, then, can the love of God abide in him who possesses worldly goods, and, seeing his brother in need, closes his heart to him?" "Everyone who loves the parent loves his child also. We know by this sign that we love the children of God: when we love God and keep his commandments." Here St. John has related the twofold commandment in a unique way. Just previously, in 4:20-21, he said that we know that we love God if we love our neighbor. Now his test of true love of neighbor is an unfeigned love of God, all of which emphasizes the unavoidable fact that the command to love is in reality one, not a divided thing. God is love, the child of God, therefore, loves God in himself and in his neighbor, and the neighbor because of God. And sin is the opposite of love: "Yes, to love God means to keep his commandments."[8]

Not only is sin contrary to the very nature of the Father and to our status as his adopted children, it is also an offense against his paternal love for us. "See what kind of love the Father has bestowed on us…." "And we ourselves have seen and now testify that the Father has sent his Son to save the world…. And we ourselves know and believe in God's enduring love at work among us." The Father is the source of all good things for us, as union with him and the Son is our end. "To you we proclaim what we have seen and heard, that you may share our treasure with us. That treasure is union with the Father and his Son, Jesus Christ." The condition of this union is faith in the Sonship of Christ, and, therefore, in his revelation of the Father and of his will: "If what you have heard from the beginning abides with you, you too will abide in the Son and in the Father. And this is what he has promised us, life eternal."[9]

The Son has come to destroy sin. We have seen the fundamental opposition of sin to Christ, but what of its particular opposition to the Spirit? To answer this we must take account of a word that St. John often uses, the "world." This "world," which St. Paul wrote of in an uncomplimentary sense, fares even worse with John. By it he designated creation that had separated itself or had been separated from God, either people, or the things, which they had perverted from their true end. Hence, St. John's world would be considered as hostile to God, not simply neutral—a whole milieu of open and deliberate antagonism. The world, although not in itself sin, is the result of and the atmosphere of sin.

> Do not love the world or what the world has to offer. If anyone loves the world, he has no love for the Father, because all that the world has to offer is the cravings that arise from what we see and a vain display in one's mode of life. These come not from the Father, but from the world.[10]

The world, therefore, is inimical to the Christian: "Do not be surprised, brothers, if the world hates you." Christ had already foretold this at his discourse after the Last Supper: "If the world hates you, bear in mind that it has hated me first. If you were children of the world, the world would cherish its own flesh and blood. But you are not children of the world; on the contrary, I have singled you out from the world, and therefore the world hates you."[11]

But because of its enmity, its very contrariness to God, the world is a grave source of sin to the Christian. Christ promised the Holy Spirit, who would be not only intercessor, but also helper against the world. But his coming would be contingent on the Christian's keeping God's commandments: "If you love me, you will treasure my commandments. And I will ask the Father, and he will grant you another Advocate to be with you for all time to come, the Spirit of Truth! The world is incapable of receiving him, because it neither sees him or knows him." Once he has come he makes victory possible, first, because as a witness to Christ he gives and strengthens faith: "The Spirit also continually bears reliable witness, because the Spirit is Truth. And so, we have three reliable witnesses of victory: the Spirit, the water, and the blood, and these three are in agreement." The Spirit, together with baptism and the Eucharist, is proof for the Christian against the world and its assaults. Faith in Christ, his divinity and his mission, leads in practice to the keeping of his commandments, and the Spirit dwells in the Christian as a reassuring presence:

> His commandment is this, that we should believe in the name of his Son, Jesus Christ, and love one another, as he commanded us. He who keeps his commandments abides in God and God in him. It is the Spirit abiding in

> us who gives us the assurance that God
> abides in us.[12]

From all of this we can draw only one conclusion: sin and the Christian are absolute opposites. Sin cannot exist in him. This is the reason why Christ established the sacrament of penance, to destroy sin and its roots in the Christian. As such it is the prolongation of baptism, our contact with Christ's saving death.

> My little children, I write this letter to you to
> keep you from sin. Yet if anyone should sin,
> we have an advocate with the Father, Jesus
> Christ, the Holy One. He himself is the propi-
> tiation for our sins; indeed not only for ours,
> but for those of the whole world.[13]

Only St. John recorded Christ's establishment of this sacrament. It happened, appropriately, on Easter night: "Then Jesus said to them again: 'Peace be to you! As the Father has made me his ambassador, so I am making you my ambassadors.' With this, he breathed on them and said: 'Receive the Holy Spirit. Whenever you remit any-one's sins, they are remitted; when you retain anyone's sins, they are retained.'" The Holy Spirit, union of Father and Son, is to be the sinner's union, and, if need be, reunion with them. St. John could certainly be refer-ring to sacramental confession when he wrote in his first Epistle: "If we openly confess our sins, God, true to his promises and just, forgives us our sins and cleanses us from every stain of iniquity."[14]

    The Council of Trent stated that the sacrament of penance was a tribunal, a court of justice, and that the priest was the judge.[15] We are reminded in this connection of these words of Christ after the Last Supper:

> Unless I depart the Advocate will not come to you; whereas, if I depart, I will send him to you. And when he comes, he will show the world the meaning of guilt, of innocence, and of condemnation; guilt—they do not believe in me; innocence—I am going home to the Father and you will see me no longer; condemnation—the prince of this world stands condemned.[16]

What is the relevance of this passage to the sacrament? Without forcing the matter, it is quite obvious that there is a similarity here with the passage in which Christ conferred the power of absolution (cf. Jn 20:21-23). In either case the Holy Spirit is given: in the one, as the unifying power of God; in the other, as judge. His judgment results in acquittal and condemnation, remitting and retaining. He points out to the world the true meaning of sin (the Greek word here is the usual New Testament word for *sin*), which is disbelief in and rejection of Christ—one of St. John's points in his first Epistle, as we have seen. Sin, then, is separation from God because it is separation from Christ. The Spirit declares Christ to be right, and therefore condemns Satan and his followers, who are opposed to Christ, as unconditionally wrong.

In the tribunal of the sacrament the Spirit declares innocent those who, having repented of their temporary defection from Christ, believe in him with all their hearts and renew their allegiance. Their sins are remitted. The ones he retains are those who persist because he cannot remit them. And he cannot because in this case he must condemn the sinner who will not accept Christ, with all that that means. It is a matter of black and white, for and against, right and wrong. Christ is right; those who are with him are right, and therefore acquitted. Because penance is an extension of baptism, the basic attitude of the penitent has to be that of the catechumen: total renunciation of Satan and total adherence to Christ.

Because the Church makes up one Person, as it were, with Christ, what he does the Church does, what happens to him happens to his body. So if the Spirit declares Christ to be right, it is the Church who is right, and if the reward for Christ's rightness (or righteousness) is his glory at the right hand of the Father, so will it be for the Church. Absolution from mortal sin in the sacrament of penance is restoring the penitent to the rightness of Christ, to active life in his body, and therefore to his glory. It is an eschatological act. We are a long way here from the idea of going to confession mainly so that we can "go to Communion."

This brings us to the fact that penance, while primarily and essentially an act of Christ through his Spirit is an act of the Church. It is not only *for,* but also *by* the Church. Penance is an ecclesial act. Christ gave the Spirit for forgiveness of sins directly to the Church, so God's forgiveness comes to the individual through the mediation of his body. While a perfect act of contrition can obtain forgiveness, as can baptism of desire, it is effective only because the reception of the sacrament is not possible. The minister of penance is so deputed by the Church, and not only has the power to forgive sins that the sacrament of orders gives, but also must receive a mandate from the local Church, called "faculties," to exercise that power within its confines. It may only be an assistant pastor in an insignificant hamlet who sits in the confessional, but he sits there as the Church in judgment, with power to acquit the offender.

What the offender on his side of the confessional is petitioning is not only acquittal, but also, and chiefly, a restoration of the life of the Mystical Body—in case he has lost it. Hence, he is asking for a return to the life of the Church. He has been a member all along, but lifeless and atrophied and useless. By his defection he has harmed the Church, for a body cannot be considered well and sound if it has one incapacitated part. The penitent has sinned against the Church as well as God, and he humbly asks to be reinstated. What an action of universal proportions takes place in a confessional in five minutes!

Fr. Anciaux, writing recently on penance, says:

> If we want to express the nature of the sacrament accurately we must keep in mind this twofold aspect of the Church's action. Ecclesiastical penance is both judgment and pardon. It is condemnation and expiation. Through both of these together, the sinner is led to reconciliation. Ecclesiastical penance is thus absolution and liberation, restitution of friendship with God by means of the restoration

> of communion in Christ. But this reconcilia-
> tion with God in Christ is the result of the
> *actio poenitentiae,* of the expiation imposed
> and hallowed by the Church. In our time, it is
> confession that forms the chief "penance"
> imposed by the Church on the sinner. The
> work of satisfaction indicated by the priest is
> its complement of expiation, and this often
> takes the form of what may be truly called an
> "indulgence."[17]

We are so accustomed today to accent the confession part of the sacrament that we fail to understand why it has traditionally been called the sacrament of penance. The earlier Church put much emphasis upon the penance element, and books were drawn up which detailed specific works of expiation for specific sins. We have only to recall that one of the origins of Lent was a time for sinners to prepare for reconciliation with God and the Church on Holy Thursday, by faithfully performing a prescribed penance. If the Old Testament can be called a history of the sin of God's people, it can also be a history of their penances by which they hoped to obtain his forgiveness.

But besides the idea of expiation, there was another underlying Old Testament and early Church penances. That was that the fasting, public humiliation, or whatever the penance might be, indicated to God and the community the truly wretched state of the sinner, cut off as he was from God and community. Also, it made him acutely aware of his own misery. It was a declaration to all concerned that sin wrought the greatest evil that a person could suffer—separation from God—and that the sinner was indeed suffering it.[18]

Today the greatest penance that the Church demands of the sinner is confession, as we have seen, and Fr. Worden elaborates on this fact:

> The absence of sackcloth and ashes, of fasting and weeping, is the reason why the name Penance seems something of a misnomer, but the name Confession draws attention to that element in the sacramental rite which plays the same part as penitential practices. The explicit confession of sins to the priest is the essential penitential practice demanded by the Church.... The confession of sins is the sinner's declaration of the evils, which have come upon him through sin, and it is his public humiliation. Through this humiliation the sinner moves God to pity and displays his miserable state to the Church.[19]

The outward sign of the sacrament of penance is the action of both penitent and priest. While sins are its remote matter, "...the proximate matter of this sacrament consists in the acts of the penitent, the matter of which acts are the sins over which he grieves, which he confesses, and for which he satisfies."[20] We can say that it is what the penitent does under the influence of divine grace, and would certainly include his contrition, which is the most important thing demanded of him in this sacrament. The whole act of sacramental confession, then, with all that it includes—expiation, contrition, and confession—is the sacramental matter.

The form is what gives the sacramental meaning, its meaning as symbolic action, and in penance the words of absolution are the form. The purpose of the penitent's act is forgiveness and acquittal. This is what the sacrament signifies, this is Christ's purpose, which is applied to the matter by means of the words, "I absolve thee."[21] It is interesting, as well as instructive, to note that only in this sacrament is there such a collaboration between priest and recipient that the one necessarily supplies the matter, the other, the form of the whole sacramental sign. It should make the penitent aware of the importance of his contribution, that not only must he be careful in confessing his sins, but also use God's grace to have the greatest contrition for them.

Since the sacrament of penance is second baptism, its particular aim is the destruction of sin. Therefore its grace has the same aim. It is true, the sacrament forgives, acquits, but the grace which it gives at the moment of acquittal has to bear a relation to sin. It has to destroy all sin in the penitent, not just the ones which he has confessed and been absolved from, but sin, as the opposite of God, as absence of God. The sanctifying grace of this sacrament is a share in the divine life that has to choose God and cannot choose any other object. It is grace that aims not at sinlessness as a negation, but at the divine activity of God. Thus in the future the penitent has a basis for sinlessness. The actual graces to which penance gives him a title are the power of God giving him the ability to choose God always, "tailored" to him as an individual, with his particular temptations and circumstances. And they certainly are directed to removing the very roots of his sins.

Given on Easter night, the sacrament of penance belongs in the framework of Easter, and no matter when it occurs in the life of the Christian, it recalls the condition, the state, of the risen Christ. For he gave it to preserve in his body his risen life.

Notes

1.   Is 53:6.
2.   Jn 1:4; 8:12; 1:5; 3:19; 1 Jn 1:5-6.
3.   1 Jn 2:20-22; Jn 1:14; 18:37; 1 Jn 2:4.
4.   1 Jn 3:5-6, 8.
5.   Jacques Guillet, *Themes of the Bible* (Notre Dame, Ind.: Fides, 1960), p. 130. The passage quoted can be found, for example, in Dt 12:31; 17:1; 18:12.
6.   1 Jn 3:3-4; 5:17; Rom 1:18. Cf. W.F. Arndt and F.W. Gingrich, *A Greek-English Lexicon of the New Testament* (Chicago: The University of Chicago Press, 1963).
7.   1 Jn 2:29; 3:1, 9-10; 5:18.
8.   1 Jn 4:7-8; 2:11; 3:15-17; 5:2-3.
9.   1 Jn 3:1; 4:14, 16; 1:3; 2:24-25.
10.   1 Jn 2:15-16.
11.   1 Jn 3:13; Jn 15:18-19.
12.   Jn 14:16-17; 1 Jn 5:6-8; 3:23-24.
13.   Jn 2:1-2.
14.   Jn 20:21-23; 1 Jn 1:9.
15.   Cf. Paul J. Palmer, S.J., ed., *Sacraments and Forgiveness* (Westminster, Md.: The Newman Press, 1959), pp. 241, 247-248.
16.   Jn 16:7-11; cf. Rudolf Schnackenburg, *New Testament Theology Today* (New York: Herder and Herder, 1963), p. 102.
17.   Paul Anciaux, *The Sacrament of Penance* (New York: Sheed and Ward, 1962), pp. 79-80.
18.   Cf. T. Worden, "The Remission of Sins—II," *Scripture,* October, 1957, pp. 120-121.
19.   *Ibid.,* pp. 126-127.
20.   *Summa Theologiae,* III, Q. 84, a. 2.
21.   *Ibid.,* a. 3.

FOURTEEN

The Anointing of the Sick: Breaking a Hold of Satan

Sickness, the loss of health, is a result of the general breakdown of man that was a punishment from God for the sin of Adam. Before we can profitably study the sacrament of the sick we should, as we did in the past chapter, attempt some theology of its subject, drawn from the New Testament.

Is all we can say of sickness, whether bodily or mental, that it results from natural causes (granting the general cause of punishment)? What do the Gospels have to tell us? For one thing they make it plain that Christ devoted much time and energy to healing the sick. For example, St. Matthew:

> And so Jesus toured the whole of Galilee, instructing the people in their synagogues and preaching the Good News of the kingdom, besides healing every disease and every infirmity found among his countrymen. The result

> was that the report about him spread to every
> place in Syria. And all those suffering from
> various diseases were brought to him,
> whether they were racked with pain, or pos-
> sessed by demons, or epileptic, or paralyzed.
> And he cured them.[1]

The instances given here could be multiplied many times, as anyone knows who has read the Gospels.

Besides his own work of healing Christ gave this power to his Apostles and sent them out on a missionary journey similar to his own. "He then called to him his twelve apostles and gave them power to drive out unclean spirits, as well as power to heal any disease and any infirmity." Note here that Christ gave them not only the power to cure from sickness, but also that to expel "unclean spirits." In the parallel passage in St. Mark the latter is the only one that is mentioned, although the Apostles "...cured many sick persons by anointing them with oil." But St. Luke's account of the same event spec-ifies both powers, only here that of exorcism is "author-ity over all the demons."[2]

Who or what are these spirits and demons? And is there a relation between them and sickness? As to the first question, the New Testament abounds in a variety of words to express Satan and his devils. Such are the above words, plus principalities, powers, virtues, prince of this world, princes, lords, gods, and elements. These are all generally interchangeable, as the various authors have their preferences, but they all mean the devils.[3] At this point it would be a good thing to rid ourselves forever of the popular caricature of Satan. He and the devils are pure spirits; therefore they have no material form, certainly not horns, cloven hooves, and a tail. If there is any "image" which the public relations department of hell would like to propagate, it is that of devils being so endowed, for such an image is quite ridiculous and, therefore, unbelievable. Instead, let us reaffirm, if need be, our belief in them, and that they are most active, hostile to God, and have one aim with regard to creation, to pervert it to themselves. The sneering adjectives, "quaint," "medieval," "unscientific," applied to belief in devils, are themselves inventions and weapons of the devils.

As to their relation with sickness, we are reminded of the woman whom Christ cured who "...for eighteen years, had been suffering from an infirmity caused by a spirit..." also of the "...demoniac who was blind and dumb...." Christ himself said of the former that Satan had bound her for eighteen years. St. Luke tells us: "He was accompanied by the Twelve, as well as by certain women who had been cured of evil spirits and infirmities...."[4] The sense here is that these spirits had caused the infirmities.[5] "These expressions draw attention to what underlies the fact of illness," writes Heinrich Schlier. "No matter what physical or psychic causes it may have, illness also is due to a superior evil power. The incidence of illness may seem fortuitous to men, but it is due to the calculated action of the superior wicked power: though this action is deliberate, man cannot predict it. This superior power has its being, not only in the impairment of the body, but also in the confusion and ruin of the spirit."[6]

This is a bit strong, and we don't have to go as far as Schlier does in ascribing all sickness to the devils. Yet there certainly is the possibility, and we must be well aware of it. If they cause some sickness, and our own fits into that "some," the phenomenon strikes home. After all, why did Christ link the power of healing with that of driving out devils? Do both go together because devils and sickness are both present?

Several of the persons whom the evangelists describe as having an "unclean spirit" strike us as acute mental cases. Not that their illness was imaginary, but clearly caused by the presence within them of a devil. If the devils can cause illness, what a field day they must have with those persons who are more susceptible to neuroses and psychoses! The very possibility of such being the case should make us realize that therapy alone may not work the cure, that there should be added the "prayer and fasting,"[7] of the patient, if possible, and certainly of the therapist and those interested.

When St. John the Baptist sent two disciples to Christ with the question, "Are you the one who is to come?" Christ answered them in words that not only combined certain prophecies of Isaiah, but also summed up his recent activities; "Go and bring word to John about all you see and hear: the blind recover sight, the lame walk, lepers are made clean, the deaf hear, dead men rise again, the humble have the Good News preached to them...." Joined to his preaching was his healing, and, as we can gather from the following passage, his driving out devils:

> "Let us go elsewhere and visit the neighboring hamlets. I want to preach there also. That is the purpose of my mission." So he went through the length and breadth of Galilee to preach in their synagogues and drive out demons.[8]

The coming of Christ into a place was the coming of his reign and of his triumph over Satan and the powers of hell. He beat the devils at every turn, in every area where they held ground. They triumphed over the sick, for they used sickness to further break down the person, already weakened in his loss of integrity, to turn his attention to his malady, and thus keep him concentrated on self. Sickness, whether caused by devils or not, would be a perfect area for diabolical operation. While the evangelists' purpose in narrating Christ's healing was to demonstrate his power, Christ's purpose was not only to fulfill prophecies and prove his mission, but also to break the kingdom of Satan.

We are struck by the relation between faith and healing in the gospel accounts of Christ's miracles, and this relation has meaning for our inquiry. "When Jesus saw their faith..." refers to that of the four men who let a paralytic down through the roof. "Go home," he said to the blind Bartimaeus, "your faith has cured you." We are familiar with the words of the centurion, asking Christ for a cure for his slave: "I am not fit to have you come under my roof.... No, utter a word and cure my slave."

Christ's reply to this was: "I tell you, I have not found such lively faith even in Israel." To the woman who touched the fringe of his cloak he said: "My daughter, your faith has cured you." And when he returned to Nazareth and its environs, St. Matthew closes his account of the visit with these revealing words: "And owing to their unbelief he did not work many miracles there."

So we see that there is at least an implied link between the devils and sickness, that Christ devoted himself to driving out devils and to healing, and that cures depended on the faith, either of the sick person or of his petitioners. (I abstract here from the cases that would not be cured because of some purpose of the divine will.) Christ's efforts were expended in spreading his kingdom and its effects. In his healing work he was breaking the hold of Satan over the sick, by restoring them to health for their supernatural good. These words of Acts sum up the matter very well: "You know how God anointed him with the Holy Spirit and with power, and he went about doing good and healing all who were in the power of the devil because God was with him."[10]

But what of this phase of Christ's ministry in the life of the Church? Sickness is still with us, with all our science, and the healing power of Christ should be applied to it. He has provided for the other areas of life; what of this important one? Christ has done so in the sacrament of the anointing of the sick.

From the available documents, such as rituals, we learn that this sacrament was given to anyone who had any kind of sickness, even mental. For instance, the prayer for blessing oil of the sick found in the ritual of the fourth-century Egyptian bishop Serapion asks that "...it may become a means of removing 'every disease and every sickness,' of warding off every demon, of putting to flight every unclean spirit, of keeping at a distance every evil spirit, of banishing all fever, all chill, and all weariness...unto health and soundness of soul and body and spirit, unto perfect well-being." And the eighth-century Gelasian Sacramentary contains more succinctly the same idea in its blessing of this oil: "And may Thy blessing be to all who anoint, taste and touch a protection for body, soul and spirit, for dispelling all sufferings, all sickness, all illness of mind and body."[11]

In the ninth century, among Charlemagne's reforms, we get the first indication that the anointing of the sick was to be considered as a rite for the dying, although it was given to the ordinary sick as before. However, this new aspect of the sacrament prevailed. "By the middle of the thirteenth century, unction, if received at all, was normally postponed until the moment of death, when all hope of recovery was lost."[12] The Council of Trent declared in 1551: "...this annointing is to be used for the sick, but especially for those who are so danger-ously ill as to appear at the point of departing this life; hence, it is also called a sacrament of the departing."[13] While this decree restored the idea of anointing the sick, its tone, as well as that of the Council's other legislation on the sacrament, emphasized its use for the dying. In the centuries since, the sacrament, known for some time as extreme unction (the last anointing), was given with more latitude than it had been in the previous three centuries, but the people came to associate it with death. Today, when we hear of anyone being "anointed," some consider him as good as dead.

It is really more traditional to call this sacrament the anointing of the sick because it is meant for more than the dying. How sick one has to be we shall discuss later. For the time being let us think of it in its original meaning.

While it can be argued that the passage already quoted, Mark 6:13, indicates Christ's institution of the sacrament, it is clear from these words of St. James: "Is anyone of you sick? He should call in the presbyters of the Church, and have them pray over him, while they anoint him with oil in the name of the Lord. That prayer, said with faith, will save the sick person, and the Lord will restore him to health. If he has committed sins, they will be forgiven him."[14] Here we have the healing ministry of Christ, as well as the elements of the sacrament. The purpose of both is a restoration to health, and this depends on faith, especially the faith of those who give the sacrament. It is only logical that we include here the ones who "call in the presbyters." The faith of all combined can effect a cure.

St. James's instruction gives us the sacramental sign, which is an anointing with oil joined to prayer. Today the oil is the third of the Church's sacred oils, that of the sick, blessed, with the others, by the bishop on Holy Thursday. It is the matter of the sacrament. The form is the prayer which the priest says as he anoints the senses and feet of the sick person: "Through this holy anointing and his most loving mercy, may the Lord forgive you whatever sins you have committed through sight, etc." The prayers that follow ask for health and healing, both interior and exterior. This is the symbolic action that is the Church's contact with Christ's healing, by which it is made present.

The chief purpose of the sacrament, from all that has been said, is health, recovery from sickness. Yet, when we consider what a sacrament is, a symbolic action that gives grace, there is a contradiction here. Health is natural. The life of grace is supernatural; so the object of the anointing of the sick has to be the giving of sacramental grace. An authority on the subject, Fr. Zoltan Alszeghy, has written on this point: "Now the help that God gives man to save him when he is sick is tailored to man as he is. In the letter of St. James the fundamental category is the whole sick man who receives not two distinct helps, but only one. Besides, the categories of body and soul, by no means basic to Hebraic thought, are not applied by St. James to the salvation of the sick."[15]

You will recall from Chapter 2 that according to the biblical concept man is not *divided* into body and soul, but *composed* of these elements, in such a way as to achieve an interrelated unity. St. James, writing as a Jew, would have this concept. And nothing could be more true, as our own experience can testify. The body certainly reacts on the soul, just as the soul reacts on the body. When we *feel* good, isn't it much easier to *be* good?

Doesn't sickness weigh down the spiritual life? For instance, how difficult it is to pray when we're sick, even though we have so much time for it. Body and soul are indeed a unity.

Sickness can have, then, two bad effects on the life of the soul: an absorption in self, a selfishness, that results in peevishness, a demanding temper, all forms of uncharity; then there is the lethargy, the sluggishness, that impedes the movements of man toward God, like a wounded body that can't get off the ground. We can see what use the devils can make of sickness, for such a condition provides them a climate in which they can thrive, with nature a ready ally against supernature. However, there can be a third, and worse, effect, and that is sin. A sick person, weakened as he is, is prone to temptations and falls. True, because of his condition, the malice of his sins may be lessened, and, perhaps, a requirement for committing a mortal sin may be absent, yet harm has been done. He has, or thinks he has, turned from God, when he otherwise wouldn't. Hell is triumphant, and the person, because of his condition, is discouraged and impatient with himself.

When Adam had the gift of integrity his soul controlled his body in a unity that was harmony. He had perfect health. His descendants, without this gift, so often find themselves at the mercy of their bodies and their passions. Sickness, with its attendant ills, bears this out. These considerations should help us to understand what Fr. Alszeghy calls the one help of the sacrament of the sick. "Applying all this to the sacramental grace of extreme unction, we can define it as *a help granted to the whole person to enable him to live intensely his supernatural life, notwithstanding the special encumbrance of sickness.*"[16]

The health that is the object of the sacrament is a restoration, in some degree, of integrity, in that a person is enabled to triumph over his ailing body. As Fr. Davis wrote:

> Consequently, the sacramental grace of this sacrament can best be seen as strength and relief given to the sick person to live a full supernatural life, despite his sickness. This grace is given to man as a living unity of body and soul and has repercussions, spiritual and bodily, throughout the whole person. On the bodily side, it implies a restoration of order and unity that might—and often does—involve a cure in the medical sense.[17]

The object is not essentially a medical cure, but a recovery that is in reality the sick person's recovery of his ability to live his supernatural life. If a cure is needed for this, a cure will be given, provided that the sacrament is given "with faith." Often a cure will be forthcoming as a result of a person's recovering his self-mastery, when there are psychosomatic elements in his sickness.

The need for faith in this sacrament has been mentioned several times in our considerations, and, perhaps, to some this smacks of "faith healing." It is not quite the same thing, for we are demanding faith in the efficacy of a sacrament. Yet a real and great faith is necessary. Concerning the recovery of health as an effect of the anointing of the sick, the *Catechism of the Council of Trent,* 1597, put it bluntly: "And if in our days the sick obtain this effect less frequently, this is to be attributed, not to any defect of the Sacrament, but rather to the weaker faith of a great part of those who are anointed with the sacred oil, or by whom it is administered...."[18] It gives for reason Christ's demand for faith in his curative power, as instanced by St. Matthew: "And owing to their unbelief he did not work many miracles there."[19] If there was a definite relation between the faith of the petitioners and a cure by Christ, as we have seen, there must still be that same relation, for it is Christ who is still operating by means of the sacrament. The anointing is his means of making his work present.

Sacramental grace is essentially sanctifying grace, directed to the effect that the sacrament is intended to achieve. So this grace that the anointing of the sick gives is the nature that enables the sufferer to live a supernatural life that is triumphant over the debilitating tendencies of his sickness. Action proceeds from nature. It is like the sanctifying grace in the suffering Christ, always enabling him to have control and to fix his human will on his Father's, exemplified so graphically in the agony in the garden and on the cross. Christ still maintained his integrity, as man he acted as the Son, to the end. Hence, the grace of the sacrament makes it possible for us not only to suffer as sons, but to act as sons, in spite of suffering and weakness, to the end.

What about the forgiveness of sins as an effect of this sacrament? It is mentioned by St. James, and the form of the sacrament clearly asks for it. If we read the text of St. James carefully, we note that this is not the chief effect—that is, the restoration to health. Forgiveness is, as it were, a "by-product." "*If* he has committed sins, they will be forgiven him." This is properly the field of the sacrament of penance, which, in practice, is given before that of anointing. However, in view of the Apostle's words, any venial sins the sufferer may have are forgiven, and, if he is unconscious, also his unforgiven mortal sins, provided that when he was conscious he was sorry for them.[20]

How sick does one have to be in order to receive this anointing? Pope Pius XI cleared up the matter in a letter to the Bona Mors Sodality in 1923:

> We are particularly anxious to enlist the eager willingness of sodalists and especially of the zealous to dispel in every way possible the deadly error which, to the detriment of souls, has given rise to the practice of not anointing the sick with holy oil, until death is imminent and they have all but lost, or lost altogether, their faculties. For it is not necessary either for the validity of the sacrament that death be feared as something proximate; rather, it is enough that there should be a prudent or probable judgment of danger. And if in such conditions unction ought to be granted, in the same conditions it surely can be granted.[21]

The distinction to be made here is between the words *proximate* and *probable*. In the first case, death is near, the person is dying; in the second, the sickness could probably result in his death. "And, to remove all anxiety in our use of this sacrament," writes Fr. Davis, "we can point to reliable moral teaching that the danger need not be objectively real for the validity of the sacrament; all is well, if we prudently think there is such danger and in doubtful cases the anointing can be validly and lawfully given."[22]

The sacrament of the dying is viaticum, the Eucharist as food for the journey to the beatific vision. But the anointing, when it is given to the dying, gives the grace to see death as the risen Christ sees it, as conquered, as in reality only a temporary stage in the Christian's life, and therefore not really death.

For death is something final, it is the end, like the end of a play or story. As such it is intimately associated with Satan, who is forever dead to the beatific vision, for whom eternal union with God, for which he was created, is irrevocably lost. Hence, he deals in death, makes use of it, and, something we do not realize, makes us preoccupied with it, fascinated as with a mystery. What he wants is for man to regard death as final, to lose hope. The slogans, "For tomorrow we die" and "You're a long time dead," are examples of such an attitude. Recent novelists have provided us with studies of such a pessimistic fascination.[23]

But deaths for the Christian and for the world are two different things. The Christian tends to put the word in quotation marks, because it is for him only quasi-death.

> Therefore, because his [Christ's] children have blood and flesh in common, he in like manner partook of these that through death he might destroy him who had control over death, that is, the devil, and deliver those whom throughout their lives the fear of death held in bondage.[24]

Satan's great spheres of operation are sin, sickness, and death. The victory of Christ over all three is made present for us personally in the sacraments, and we have seen how this is particularly so in penance and the anointing of the sick. Every reception of these sacraments should make us exult with the words of St. Paul: "But thanks be to God, who gives us the victory through our Lord Jesus Christ."[25] But more important than our own victory is the personal triumph of Christ. Every absolution given, every anointing is Christ coming into the territory of Satan to break his hold. It is the presence in the world of the victory of Christ over Satan.

Notes

1. Mt 4:23-24.
2. Mt 10:1; Mk 6:7, 13; Lk 9:1.
3. Cf. Heinrich Schlier, *Principalities and Powers in the New Testament* (New York: Herder and Herder, 1961), pp. 11-15. The book belongs to Herder and Herder's "Disputed Questions" series.
4. Lk 13:11; Mt 12:22; Lk 13:16; 8:2. Cf. Mk 9:17-27.
5. So W.F. Arndt and F.W. Gingrich, *A Greek-English Lexicon of the New Testament* (Chicago: The University of Chicago Press, 1963), "Astheneia," p. 114.
6. Schlier, *op. cit.,* p. 22.

7.   Mk 9:29.

8.   Lk 7:22. Cf. Is 35:5-6; 61:1; Mk 1:38-39.

9.   Mk 2:5; 10:52; Lk 7:6, 9; 8:48; Mt 13:58.

10.   Acts 10:38.

11.   Paul F. Palmer, S.J., ed., *Sacraments and Forgiveness* (Westminster, Md.: The Newman Press, 1962), pp. 280, 288.

12.   Paul F. Palmer, S.J., "The Purpose of Anointing the Sick: A Reappraisal," *Theological Studies,* September, 1958, p. 330. Cf. pp. 314-342.

13.   *Ibid.,* p. 312.

14.   Jas 5:14-15.

15.   Zoltan Alszeghy, S.J., "The Bodily Effects of Extreme Unction," *Theology Digest,* Spring, 1961, p. 107.

16.   *Ibid.,* p. 109. The italics are the translator's.

17.   Charles Davis, *Theology for Today* (New York: Sheed and Ward, 1962), p. 267.

18.   In Palmer, ed., *Sacraments and Forgiveness,* pp. 315-316.

19.   Mt 13:58.

20.   Cf. A. Tanquerey, *A Manual of Dogmatic Theology* (New York: Desclée Company, 1957), Vol. II, p. 346.

21.   In Palmer, ed., *Sacraments and Forgiveness,* p. 320.

22.   Davis, *op. cit.,* p. 266.

23.   Cf. Schlier, *op. cit.,* pp. 33-34.

24.   Heb 2:14-15.

25.   1 Cor 15:57.

CHAPTER FIFTEEN

Holy Orders: For the Increase of Sons

Two sacraments Christ left the Church to insure its continuance until the end of time: holy orders and matrimony. Both are sacraments of state, that is, both create a definite state of life by conferring a divine mission—increase the number of adopted sons! Both states are dedicated to spreading the kingdom of God. This concept of matrimony may strike the married reader as being a bit extreme. But remember, we are not treating of marriage as merely a contract, but of the sacrament of matrimony. The point to be made here is that orders and matrimony work together, by means of different functions, for the same end.

The very idea of priesthood is essentially related to sacrifice. This is so in every religion that has a priesthood.[1] We know the role of the Old Testament priests in the temple sacrifices: their basic function was to sacrifice. Hence, the following passages from the Epistle to the Hebrews were understood by their original readers in this context: "In fact every high priest is chosen from among men and appointed to serve men in what concerns the worship of God. He is to offer gifts and sacrifices in expiation of sins." "To this every high priest is appointed—to offer gifts and sacrifices."[2]

The great message of this epistle is that Christ is the only priest of the new covenant. A priest, because he offers sacrifice, is a mediator. But Christ alone holds the position of mediator between God and man because his is the only sacrifice.

> He has no need of offering sacrifice day by day, as do the other high priests, first for their own and then for the people's sins. He did this once for all, when he offered himself.

> But when Christ, high priest of the messianic blessings, appeared, he entered once for all through the greater and more perfect tabernacle not made by human hands, that is, not of earthly origin.

> But now once and for all in the final epoch he has presented himself to abolish sin by his sacrifice. And just as it is appointed for men to die once and then to undergo judgment, so also was Christ offered only once to bear the sins of the multitude.[3]

Christ is priest because he is the Son. The very essence of sacrifice is offering, the offering of oneself, symbolized by the victim. The sacrificial obedience of the Son made man will result in adopted sons.

> Similarly Christ did not seek for himself the glory of becoming the high priest, but God said to him: "You are my Son; today have I become your Father." So too he says in another place, "You are a priest forever after the manner of Melchisedech." Jesus, when he had a mortal body, offered prayers and supplications with piercing cries and tears to him who was able to save him from death, and he was heard because of his reverent piety. Son though he was, he learned obedience through what he suffered, and after he had been raised to the heights of perfection, he became to all who obey him the cause of eternal salvation, since God had proclaimed him a high priest after the manner of Melchisedech.[4]

But Christ still exercises his priesthood in heaven, at the right hand of the Father: "There in the sanctuary and the true tabernacle, which the Lord, and not man, has erected, he carries on priestly functions." He is *the* priest in the Church, the minister of every sacrament. The sacraments by means of symbolic acts make present Christ's past actions and the intention that was in him then to give grace by means of the sacraments, but the merit of his acts and this same intention are in him now, the glorified Christ. The merit and the intention become operative when the human agent performs the sacramental sign, active in him now with regard to the recipient of the sacrament. So Christ is truly the priest of the

Church, because he is not only the mediator who merited grace in the past, but also the mediator who bestows it now. And, too, as man he asks the Father—again as mediator, therefore as priest—to bestow it through him: "It is Jesus who died, yes, and who rose again, who is at the right hand of God, who also intercedes for us."[5]

Christ's first concern for the Church was with a priesthood that would provide human agents for his own priesthood. Thus his great care in determining and forming the Apostles, who would be the first human priests in the Church. "As the Father has made me his ambassador, so I am making you my ambassadors." "He who descended is the same one who also ascended above all the heavens, that he might fully impart all graces. He established some men as apostles, and some as inspired spokesmen, others again as evangelists, and others as pastors and teachers, thus organizing the saints for the work of the ministry, which consists in building up the body of Christ...."[6]

The Apostles, as the first priests, were necessarily bishops—having the fullness of the priesthood, a fullness imperative for "building up the body of Christ." St. Paul was bishop for all the churches he established in Asia Minor, sending auxiliary bishops, such as Timothy and Titus, to take over a church while he moved on.

The Acts and the Epistles use the words "bishop" and "presbyter" in an interchangeable sense, as in St. Paul's address to the "presbyters" of Ephesus (Acts 20:17), in which he refers to them as "bishops" (20:28). The salutation of the Epistle to the Philippians mentions only bishops and deacons. If the original bishop-presbyters had the fullness of the priesthood, it was not long before a distinction was made. St. Ignatius of Antioch gives three grades of priesthood, writing before the year 107: "See that you all follow the bishop, as Jesus Christ follows the Father, and the presbytery as if it were the Apostles. And reverence the deacons as the command of God." The bishop has preeminence over the others: "Let no one do any of the things appertaining to the Church without the bishop. Let that be considered a valid Eucharist that is celebrated by the bishop, or by one whom he appoints. Whenever the bishop appears let the congregation be present; just as wherever Jesus Christ is, there is the Catholic Church."[7]

If the Church was to continue and the Mystical Body was to be completed, the power of the priesthood had to be given by the Apostles. They were aware of this, and gave the sacrament of orders as the need arose. There are several references to "the apostles and the presbyters" at Jerusalem, an indication that the latter were early associated with the Apostles as their extensions and successors.[8] When Paul and Barnabas preached in Derbe, Lystra, Iconium, and Antioch, they ordained before their departure: "When, with the imposition of hands, they had appointed presbyters for them in each congregation after prayer and fasting, they commended them to the Lord, in whom they had believed." St. Paul admonished his auxiliary bishop, Timothy: "Do not neglect the grace of office you have, which was granted to you by inspired designation with the imposition of the presbyters' hands." Thus the Apostles insured that the redemptive work of Christ would come to "all nations," and that his presence would be in the world "as long as the world will last."[9]

When did Christ institute the sacrament of holy orders? When he commissioned the Apostles to carry out his priestly work and gave them the power to do so. Priesthood implies power and mandate. The first indication of this was the mandate: "...do this in remembrance of me." Here Christ gave the Apostles the power to make present his one sacrifice. From then on whenever an Apostle or one of his successors would pronounce the words of consecration, Christ, the one priest of the new covenant, would be present, offering to the Father his redemptive life, and especially his sacrificial death, his great act of atonement and merit. A second stage of the Apostles' ordination occurred on Easter night when Christ gave them the power to forgive sins, as we have seen in Chapter 13.[10] Again they were to be the mediators of his sacrifice, bringing its atonement and grace to the destruction of particular sins. These two stages associated the Apostles with sacrifice, therefore making them priests, but not with the multiple offerings of the old covenant but with the single sacrifice of the new.

But there is a relationship between the origin of the sacraments and Christ's sacrificial death. As Father Riga recently wrote: "As early as the apostolic period, St. John the Evangelist saw the sacraments as instituted by Christ on the cross and issuing symbolically from his wounded side."[11] He is referring to this passage: "...but one of the soldiers pierced his side with a lance, and immediately there came out blood and water." Now St. John mentions blood and water in his first Epistle: "He it is who came to make us victors by purifying and redeeming us, and by the effusion of the Spirit. He made victory possible for us not merely by the water of baptism but both by the water and by his blood. The Spirit also continually bears reliable witness, because the Spirit is Truth. And so, we have three reliable witnesses of victory: the Spirit, the water, and the blood, and these three are in agreement."[12] Commentators as far distant in time as St. Bede and Fr. Stanley, S.J., have seen in this passage references to baptism and the Eucharist. They relate it to St. John's account of the blood and water flowing from Christ's side. Father Stanley has written: "The whole sacramental orientation of the fourth Gospel... permits us to see in the water a symbol of baptism, in the blood a symbol of the Eucharist, the two sacraments which are primary 'Witnesses' to Christ's work of redemption."[13] These are only two sacraments. How can it be said that all take their origin from Christ's death, apart from the essential fact that they owe their efficacy to that death?

This is the reason for St. John's third "witness," the Spirit. When St. Matthew described Christ's death, he wrote that he "...gave up his spirit." The Greek has the sense of letting it go, releasing it. Mark and Luke stated simply that he expired. John, however, who wrote his Gospel after the others, worded it differently: "And he bowed his head and surrendered his spirit."[14] The

meaning here is handing over, transmitting. "This departure from the normal and idiomatic Greek expressions
found in the Synoptics Matthew, Mark and Luke must be
intentional on John's part. The evangelist has seen in
Jesus' last breath the first outpouring of the Spirit."[15]
The first effect of the redemptive act of Christ is giving
the Spirit. Once more I ask you to consider the basic
diagram of this book:

First Father and Son give the Spirit, merited by the Son,
who makes us adopted sons in Christ, and unites us in
him to the Father. It is the Spirit, acting as "uniter," who
is the "contact" between Christ and us in the sacraments.
Thus we can see in Christ's handing over the Spirit at
the instant of his death the giving of the vital principle of
all the sacraments.

How is this related to the priesthood? The
answer to this question should be obvious: the priest
gives the Spirit. We see this in the earliest accounts of
priestly activity. For example: "Now when the apostles in
Jerusalem heard that Samaria had accepted the word of
God, they sent Peter and John to them. On their arrival
they prayed for the Samaritans, that they might receive
the Holy Spirit.... Then Peter and John laid their hands
on them, and they received the Holy Spirit." What follows is interesting in this connection: "When Simon saw

that the Holy Spirit was imparted through the laying on of the apostles' hands, he offered them money, saying, 'Give me also this power, so that anyone on whom I lay my hands may receive the Holy Spirit.'" St. Paul wrote to the Corinthians that his ministry to them was the work of the Spirit: "...you are evidently a letter from Christ, drawn up by us, written not with ink but with the Spirit of the living God, not on tablets of stone but on tablets of the human heart."[16]

The Spirit gives the redemption of Christ through the sacraments; the priest is merely his agent. Thus the priest must be a man of the Spirit, filled with him in a special way for this mission. "Receive the Holy Spirit," Christ said to the Apostles on Easter night when he gave them the power to forgive sins. First the priest must have the Spirit if he is to give him to others. Christ symbolized his gift of the Spirit by breathing on the Apostles, an action that the priest performs on the baptismal water and on the person to be baptized. The Apostles looked for a symbolic action in the Old Testament and conferred the Spirit upon ordinands by the imposition, or laying on, of hands. Today this action is done in silence, although such has not always been the case. A Pontifical used in Toulouse about 1300 notes that in some places when the bishop lays his hands on the head of the ordinand he says, "Receive the Holy Spirit," with the rest of the passage (Jn 20:23).[17]

Besides being a man of the Spirit the priest must truly be another Christ, or, to speak more correctly, he must be, as far as this is possible, Christ, visible and audible. As Christ is the image of the invisible God, the priest must be the image of the invisible Christ. For this he receives at ordination a special character. We have considered the characters of baptism and confirmation as sealing us with the image of Christ. The grace of these sacraments gives us the ability to fill in the general image. These characters are similar to the "anointing" of Christ's human nature by the divine at the instant of his incarnation, in that they confer Christ upon us with his life, to be lived in preference to our own. We can say that they "place" us in the Mystical Body, because they confer on us our function in the whole Christ: that of baptism stamps us with the image of the incarnate Son, that of confirmation, with that of the redeeming Son. So the character of holy orders is an identification of the man with Christ for the fullness of his priestly work, an identification with Christ the priest.

The priesthood of the laity, which the characters of baptism and confirmation confer and develop, gives the lay person the power to be offered by the priest and to offer through him at Mass, but it does not make him the mediator of offering. Only the priest is the mediator between God and man, who makes the God-man present on the altar as the priest. The characters, which the layman has received, make it possible for him to be offered with Christ the victim, because he is actually *in* Christ the head, and therefore he can offer Christ, because he is a member of Christ. But he is not Christ the priest. Only one who has received this identification can stand at the altar and by right join his offering of Christ to the Father with that of the present Christ. The master of cere-

Holy Orders: For the Increase of Sons

monies, standing alongside the priest, may say with him
silently the prayers of the canon, but his offering has
validity only through that of the one who has received
the image of Christ the priest. I have said that the sacramental characters "place" us in the Mystical Body,
according to the functions they confer. Sociologists would
call this "stratification." The result of this for the Church
is hierarchy.

Fr. Scheeben had much to say of the sacramental
character. I abstract one passage that is pertinent to
our topic:

> In a physical body all the members are
> related by a common similarity and union
> with the head, even though such similarity
> and union may vary considerably. Likewise
> the sacramental character varies in form,
> according as it has to shape only the ordinary
> members which merely have part in the fel-
> lowship of the head [baptism], or the active
> members in which the head is to fight and
> struggle [confirmation], or the special organs
> of the head that are to bring about and to sus-
> tain the union of the rest of the members with
> the head.[18]

Fr. Bligh sees the chief function of the priesthood as
Scheeben did, referring to Ephesians 4:11-12, already
quoted in this chapter:

> All the powers of the priesthood are given for
> the one purpose of sanctifying God's people,
> building up or "edifying" the Mystical Body of
> Christ. The power of consecrating the

> Eucharist is no less for this purpose than the power of absolution, because the Blessed Sacrament is the sacrament of unity and the source of cohesion in the Mystical Body.[19]

All the priest's powers are directed to giving the Spirit, who adopts sons for the Father, through and in Christ, and who fulfills in them the measure of sonship willed for them by the Father. Thus while the priest can actualize the sacraments, he is merely the human agent of Christ and the Spirit who, by means of the sacraments, are building up the whole Christ, forming the members into the image of the Son. Mediator he is, but mediator for this divine activity on the one hand, and for human activity to meet the divine, on the other.

The sacramental sign of holy orders is the imposition of the bishop's hands on the ordinand's head. This sign derives from the Apostles, who, as I have said above, took it from the Old Testament. There it meant that a person was thereby designated for some specific purpose, or, when the priest laid his hand on the head of the victim, that that particular animal was set apart to be a victim of sacrifice. So in orders it designates the man to receive the priesthood, and is the *matter* of the sacrament. The *form*, which gives meaning to this symbolic act, is the long prayer called the preface of consecration, which the bishop says after the imposition. These together confer the sacrament. There follow other actions in the ordination rite—giving the priestly vestments, the chalice and paten, anointing the new ordained hands— but these derive their meaning and validity from the actual ordination, which is the imposition of the bishop's hands and the subsequent preface.[20]

So far no mention has been made of bishops as partaking of this sacrament, except in the early Church. What I have said has been about the priesthood as a state conferred by the sacrament of holy orders, whose mission is to build the Mystical Body. All of this has included the bishops, has applied to them more particularly, for they alone receive the fullness of the priesthood. Priests as such share in this fullness.

The bishops are the true successors of the Apostles. The latter received their priestly ordination at the Last Supper and on Easter night, and their episcopal consecration on Pentecost, when the "imposition of hands" was the descent upon their heads of the Spirit under the sign of tongues of fire.[21] Episcopal consecration gives the candidate this pentecostal gift. That it gives the fullness of priesthood can be seen in instances in past centuries when, say, a deacon was consecrated a bishop, without having been ordained a priest first. (The practice of the Church today is to give the consecration only to one who is already a priest.)

What I have said earlier in this chapter about the priestly character being an identification with Christ the priest certainly applies to bishops. But a distinction must be made. The priest receives one character at his ordination, the bishop, another at his consecration. To be quite correct, that of the bishop is the *complete* character of priesthood, whereas that of the priest is a share in it.

The character that the bishop receives derives strictly from the messianic character of "the anointed," Christ. It confers on him *ex officio,* by right of office, the messianic work of Christ. Thus, the sacrament of orders is intimately related to that of confirmation, which confers messiahship as *participation* by the laity in the public life and work of Christ. But here no participation in some degree is given, but the *fullness* of Christ's work. Therefore the bishop's character is that of the messiah—priest, king, and prophet.

> In the formula of episcopal consecration the Church asks: "Bring to completion in your priest the fullness of your ministry." In virtue of the character the bishop is configured or likened to Christ in his threefold priestly role as priest, prophet, and king. As priest, the bishop has the power to offer the Eucharistic sacrifice and to forgive sins. As prophet, he has the office *ex officio* of teaching and preaching. As king he has the full pastoral charge of guiding the flock entrusted to his care.[22]

The character of ordination makes one a priest and gives him a share in the messianic ministry of the bishop. That is, he is officially a priest, with the power to offer the sacrifice of the new covenant, to be the mediator between God and man, and he is able to be king and prophet in subordination to the bishop, who has these latter two offices by divine commission, and the priesthood in its fullness. The priest exercises his priestly ministry as auxiliary and extension of the bishop. The character of priestly orders gives the power to be the mediator of sacramental grace for the Mystical Body; the bishop can restrict, but he cannot take away this power. However, only the character of episcopal consecration gives the other messianic functions of king and prophet. Only the bishop can rule his flock as its pastor, only he is its teacher. When he delegates these functions, as he does, to his extensions, his priests are able to perform them by reason of their character as mediators.

What is the grace of the sacrament of orders? Speaking generally we can say that it is the Holy Spirit. But in this sacrament it is the Spirit who is given in order to be given by the priest. He receives the Spirit to be released by his priestly work. The priest exists for others, and the Spirit is in him for the work of giving sonship. Only secondarily is he there for the priest's own holiness. The priest is not first of all a model, but a mediator, just as Christ is not chiefly a good man, a pattern of holiness to be imitated, but *the* mediator, actively building his Mystical Body through the Spirit. As to the sanctifying grace that orders gives, it is the atmosphere, the milieu, of the Spirit coming to the newly ordained for this activity. It is the share in *his* nature, which will be the principle of action for the priest, making it possible for him and the Spirit to work in the closest cooperation for the increase of sonship.

There are three orders that are given by this sacrament, three stages, or degrees of participation in Christ's priesthood. The third is that of deacons. We learn of the institution of this order in the Acts, when the

Apostles decided that they needed helpers to distribute alms. Seven men were chosen by the congregation, among whom was St. Stephen. That the order was to be found outside of the Jerusalem church is attested by St. Paul's references to them, as well as by those of St. Ignatius.[23]

It was natural that liturgical functions should develop for the deacons. The Greek word *diakonos* originally meant "one who serves at table." The early deacons were given the task of receiving the offerings of bread and wine for the Eucharistic sacrifice. What was not needed they put aside for the poor. Thus it was a logical development that deacons were allowed to distribute the same offerings after the consecration. We are accustomed today to see deacons, in their home parishes for vacation, help the priests give Communion. The order of the diaconate early developed as not only helpers of the priests but also "middlemen" between them and the people in the liturgy. We see this in the Byzantine rites, in which the deacon stands between priest and congregation at Mass, leading the litanies. The reading of the Gospel in the Mass grew out of the preaching work that was assigned to deacons from the beginning. Both Stephen and Philip, of the original seven, preached, and this function as performed by deacons is mentioned by St. Paul.[24] Another liturgical work of the deacons has been that of giving solemn baptism, although in our day they may do this only as "extraordinary" ministers, that is, in exceptional cases. In all these duties we see the deacons as true auxiliaries of the priests, and today, as "servers of the eucharistic table."[25]

This, then, is the role of the priesthood: to build the Mystical Body, the whole Christ, until he comes, and it shall be complete. We recognize the fullness of this role in the bishops, anointed to be priests, kings, and prophets, and the participation in it by the priests, and, in their turn, by the deacons. It is the sacrament for the sacraments, which give the life of the Church.

Notes

1. E.O. James, *The Nature and Function of Priesthood* (New York: Barnes and Noble, Inc., 1955), pp. 145-175.

2. Heb 5:1; 8:3.

3. Heb 7:27; 9:11, 27-28. Cf. 10:10, 12, 14.

4. Heb 5:5-10.

5. Heb 8:2; Rom 8:34.

6. Jn 20:21; Eph 4:10-12.

7. St. Ignatius, *Epistle to the Smyrnaeans,* 8, in Kirsopp Lake, tr., *The Apostolic Fathers* (Cambridge: Harvard University Press, 1945), Vol. I, p. 261.

8. E.g., Acts 15:4, 6, 22-23.

9. Acts 14:23; 1 Tim 4:14; Mt 28:19-20.

10. 1 Cor 11:24-25; cf. Jn 20:22-23.

11. Peter Riga, *Sin and Penance* (Milwaukee: The Bruce Publishing Company, 1962), p. 146.

12. Jn 19:34; 1 Jn 5:6-8.

13. David Stanley, S.J., "The New Testament Doctrine of Baptism," *Theological Studies,* June, 1957, p. 204.

14. Mt 27:50; Mk 15:37; Lk 23:46; Jn 19:30.

15. Stanley, *loc. cit.,* pp. 204-205.

16. Acts 8:14-19; cf. also 19:1-7; 2 Cor 3:3.

17. Cf. John Bligh, S.J., *Ordination to the Priesthood* (New York: Sheed and Ward, 1956), p. 92.

18. Matthias Scheeben, *The Mysteries of Christianity* (St. Louis: Herder, 1955), p. 590.

19. Bligh, *op. cit.,* p. 18.

20.   Cf. *Acta Apostolicae Sedis,* Vol. 40 (1948), pp. 5-7.
21.   Cf. Joseph Lecuyer, C.S.S.P., *What Is a Priest?* (New York: Hawthorn Books, 1959), pp. 34-35.
22.   Paul F. Palmer, S.J., *Sacraments of Healing and of Vocation* (Englewood Cliffs, N.J.: Prentice-Hall, Inc., 1963), p. 69.23. Cf. Acts 6:1-6; Phil 1:1; 1 Tim 3:8-13; St. Ignatius, *To the Smyrnaeans,* 8:10; 12.
24.   Acts 6:8-15; 8:4-13; 1 Tim 3:13.
25.   The orders of subdeacon, acolyte, exorcist, lector, and porter do not participate in the sacrament of holy orders, even though the first is considered, with that of priest and deacon, one of the major orders, and demands celibacy and the duty of praying the Divine Office. Originally they were auxiliaries of the deacon, taking over his many duties. Today they mark stages to the priesthood, as, of course, does the diaconate.

SIXTEEN

Matrimony: Christ and the Church

Holy Orders invests men with the messianic mission of building the Mystical Body. But there is a sacrament that by its very nature is meant to be the image of that Body, and an image that is not a mere picture, but an expression in concrete form of the reality. Such is the essential nature of the sacrament of matrimony.

St. Paul has described this nature in his Epistle to the Ephesians. Although the passage is somewhat extended, I quote it in full because of its importance:

> Let wives be subject to their husbands who are representatives of the Lord, because the husband is head of the wife just as Christ is the head of the Church and also the savior of that body. Thus, just as the Church is subject to Christ, so also let wives be subject to their husbands in all things. Husbands, love your wives, just as Christ loved the Church, and

> delivered himself for her, that he might sanc-
> tify her by cleansing her in the bath of water
> with the accompanying word, in order to pres-
> ent to himself the Church in all her glory,
> devoid of blemish or wrinkle or anything of
> the kind, but that she may be holy and flaw-
> less. Even so ought husbands to love their
> wives as their own bodies. He, who loves his
> wife, loves himself. Now no one ever hates his
> own flesh; on the contrary, he nourishes and
> cherishes it, as Christ does the Church,
> because we are members of his Body. "For this
> cause a man shall leave his father and
> mother, and cling to his wife; and the two
> shall become one flesh." This is a great mys-
> tery—I mean in regard to Christ and the
> Church. Meanwhile, let each of you love his
> wife just as he loves himself, and let the wife
> reverence her husband.[1]

Christ is the first sacrament, because his human nature is the image of the invisible God, and because that nature as an outward sign contains and conveys grace. The Church is the second sacrament in that the visible Church is the sign of the Mystical Body, the grace-producing union of Christ the head and his members, and is the medium of that grace. What St. Paul is saying is that husband and wife, united in the sacrament of matrimony, are themselves a sacrament, for, like the visible Church, they are a symbol, a sign, expressing the basic reality, the Mystical Body. Their union signifies the union of Christ and his Church. The Apostle's use of the word *mystery* gives this sense to verse 32: the union of husband and wife is the revelation of the great and hidden truth of the mystico-physical oneness that exists between Christ and his members. In other words, Christian marriage teaches us what the Mystical Body is.

St. Paul is definitely not saying that marriage is *like* the Mystical Body, that it is a metaphor for it because of certain similarities. No, if we would stop at that, we would miss the whole point. Christian marriage is an image, true, but one that has an intrinsic relation to the reality it signifies. The essence of St. Paul's thought is in this passage—first the quotation from Genesis, then his interpretation of it: "'…and the two shall become one flesh.' This is a great mystery—I mean in regard to Christ and the Church."

Revelation speaks of the marriage of the Lamb, Christ, with his bride, the Church: "One of the seven angels…came and spoke to me. 'Come, I will show you the bride, the spouse of the Lamb.' Then he took me in ecstasy up to a large and high mountain, and he showed me the city of Jerusalem, coming down out of heaven from God, surrounded with the divine glory."[2] The last book of the Bible clears up the meaning of the words in the first book: "…and the two shall become one flesh," with an aid from St. Paul's comment. In the eternal mind and intention of God monogamous marriage was instituted from the beginning *because* it would be a sign of the union of Christ and the Church.

If there is any sacrament that admits of a natural interpretation, that sacrament is matrimony. And especially in our day, with birth control rampant, with moral theologians weighing secondary against primary ends, to say nothing of our Roman tendency to view the whole thing in legal terms as a contract with benefit of clergy. Too, the sacrament has become lost in the accumulation of customs that properly belong to folkways. It is extremely difficult to approach marriage from the supernatural, yet this is the only approach, for, as I said in the first chapter, there is no such thing as the isolated natural level. Seeing matrimony only on that level is seeing a mirage.

St. Paul saw Adam as a type of Christ. A type in the Bible is a person, a thing, or an action, which is really a figure of a person, thing, or action that is to come. Such, for example, is the manna, which by Christ's own authority, was a type of the Eucharist. St. Paul called Adam "... a type of him who was to come,"[3] and built on this fact to show that Christ was the head of a new race. The early Church Fathers accordingly saw Eve as a type of the Church, but not primarily because she was Adam's wife, but because she was created from a rib taken from his side while he was asleep. Here, for example, is Tertullian (died about 223) on the subject: "If Adam was a type of Christ, Adam's sleep was [a type] of the death of Christ who had slept in death. Eve coming from Adam's side is a type of the Church, the true mother of all the living."[4]

The Church was born from the side of the dead Christ by the water, baptism, and nourished on his blood, the Eucharist. This is St. John's reason for writing:

"...but one of the soldiers pierced his side with a lance, and immediately there came out blood and water,"[5] as we saw in a previous chapter. Fr. Daniélou has summed up the Fathers on this point:

> Eve, born of Adam's flesh, is the Church born of the Word made flesh, since it is first from the pierced side of Christ, sleeping on the cross, as from the pierced side of Adam, that blood and water flowed out, symbols of Baptism and Eucharist, giving birth and life to the Church—and this communication of life is continued by the sacramental life, through which the flesh of Christ received in communion continues to sanctify the Church.[6]

This is the meaning of the words of St. Paul to the Ephesians: "Husbands, love your wives, just as Christ loved the Church, and delivered himself for her, that he might sanctify her by cleansing her in the bath of water with the accompanying word...." This bath with word is, of course, baptism. So Eve, created from Adam's side, is in reality the Church, created from Christ's. When Adam first saw Eve, he said: "She now is bone of my bone, and flesh of my flesh; she shall be called Woman, for from man she has been taken." The point the sacred writer was making here was that there was a oneness between Adam and Eve because of the fact that she was created out of Adam. Here were not two people of independent origins, but the one derived from the other. No matter what the actual origin of the first man and woman, the writer of Genesis, as we know, was not relating a scientific account. He was, under the inspiration of the Holy Spirit, and in the light of the fall of man and the promise of the Messiah, relating an account that presented the types of the Messiah and his people. The people of God would be created from the side of the Redeemer, as Eve from Adam.

The passage following Adam's words appears to be the comment of the sacred writer, but actually, on Christ's authority, it was spoken by God the Creator: "For this reason a man leaves his father and mother, and clings to his wife, and the two become one flesh."[7] Is the meaning of the whole passage that a man and wife are two in one flesh because woman originally was created from man and is, therefore, really one with him because she is part of him? On the face of it, yes. The union, or bond, that marriage creates, is based radically on the original union of man and woman, akin to that existing between mother and child. But—and here we return to St. Paul and the Church Fathers—that is not the meaning at all. The whole passage, apart from what it intends to teach us about God's creation of man, means that Christ and his Church are so closely united—"two shall become one flesh"—because the Church was created from the side of the crucified Christ by baptism. Or, Christ created the Church out of himself, so that she would be totally his, and united himself to her in a union that was in reality one person—his Mystical Body. To repeat the important passage of Ephesians: "'...and the two shall become one flesh.'

This is a great mystery—I mean in regard to Christ and the Church." To conclude: according to these biblical witnesses, God instituted marriage, the union of one man and one woman until death, as a type, and later as a symbol, of the Mystical Body. First in the mind of God came the Mystical Body, and then came marriage.[8]

Therefore all monogamous marriage today is a symbol of the union of Christ and the Church, of the new Adam and the new Eve. We have to stop thinking of this type of marriage, with its forbidding of divorce and remarriage, as merely a legal thing, or something arising only out of natural law, or as an invention of the Church. Its origin, as well as meaning, is far deeper, and to understand that origin is to safeguard one's own marriage, as well as to prepare for it by a courtship that approaches the "great mystery" with day-by-day reverence and awe.

The longer passage from Ephesians quoted above is the Lesson read in the Nuptial Mass in the Latin rite, and the second prayer said after the Our Father over the bride and groom has these words: "God, who has allowed wedlock by a great sacrament, thereby foreshadowing, in the marriage bond, Christ's union with the Church...." In the Byzantine rites of the Eastern Church the couple is crowned "...in symbolic representation of the union between Christ the King and His Bride, the Holy Church."[9]

Marriage is the closest union between two human beings, as marital love is the greatest of human loves. We can view this love only from the exalted viewpoint that we have been taking. But first we must look at other unions if we are to understand the true nature of marital love. What is the closest union in existence? The Holy Trinity, in which three Persons have the one divine nature. What is the next? The hypostatic union—Christ—in which two natures are united in one divine Person. The next closest is the Mystical Body, and then comes marriage. Christ gave the principle and pattern of human unity in these words which sum up the purpose of Christianity: "All are to be one; just as you, Father, are in me and I am in you, so they, too, are to be one in us."[10] Human unity consists in being in Christ, in the one mystical Person that is the whole Christ, and entering the Trinity in him, as far as this is possible to man. Thus, at the end of time, when the Church will be complete, the closest union in existence will still be the Trinity, but it will be Father, incarnate Son with his whole body, and Spirit. The Spirit will be forever the love of the Mystical Body, for he is the love of the Son for the Father.

Love in the Mystical Body now must be primarily the Holy Spirit: "...God's love is poured forth in our hearts by the Holy Spirit who has been given us."[11] Since husband and wife form the image of the Mystical Body, this is the love they must give each other. When Christ sees his Body, the Church, he loves it not only with the love of his human will, but also, and primarily, with the love that is the Spirit, because he recognizes himself in it—"bone of my bone, and flesh of my flesh." So must the husband, who is especially the image of Christ, love his wife, whom he sees as the image of Christ's whole body, and therefore as Christ, as himself. "He who loves his wife, loves himself. Now no one ever hates his own flesh...." The wife, reverencing her husband as Christ her head, tenders him the love of the Mystical Body, the Spirit. Marital love is far from being a mere elevation and sanctification of natural love, even the best natural love. No, it is the very love of Father and Son for each other given to humans whereby they can love each other, because they have been elevated to the divine level of living. Marital love that comes from the sacrament is the Holy Spirit. He does not do away with good natural love, but builds on it, as grace on nature, directs and increases it.

The union of Christ and his Church is fruitful, dynamic, not something unproductive and static. Christ's Body is not complete; the whole Christ is not yet whole. Out of the union of Christ and his Bride come the off-spring of sons, unnumbered sons, which the Bride presents to her Spouse from out of the womb of the baptismal font. The increase of children is their first concern in their life together. Only when the number of children will be complete, will they settle down to the full enjoyment of their mature love in the long eternity. Because they are the image of Christ and his Bride, the Christian husband and wife are concerned with their part in completing the whole Christ. The increase of sons is the chief object of their life together, and proudly they present these to the Church to be born again. Thus we see a very real relation between matrimony and holy orders. Both states are dedicated to build the Mystical Body. But in orders the union is with Christ the mediator, who stands alone between God and man, whereas in matrimony the union is with the whole Christ and, more, is the expression of that ever fruitful union.

Those who have taken a primarily naturalistic view of marriage have tended to view the marriage act the same way, as basically the same thing as the reproductive act in animals. They will grant that man, having a soul, is able to regulate the act by means of his intellect and will, and they accept it as an expression of marital love, which it certainly is. They may even be able to see it as the means to increase the number of adopted sons, to build the Mystical Body. But when it comes to seeing it as an expression of the fruitfulness of Christ and his Church, Bible notwithstanding, they stop short. They cannot understand anything supernatural in the act itself. One reason for this is that they do not know the meaning of *spirit* in man. You will recall from Chapter 2 that a man's spirit is his capability for union with God, and with that supernatural union that has become possible through Christ. It is the spirit in every man that cries out for fulfillment in the Mystical Body, and ultimately in the life of the Trinity. True, man has body and soul: with the body he can reproduce like any animal, with the soul he can control reproduction as a human being. But he also has spirit, which lifts the whole thing right out of the merely human, natural, level—no matter how "civilized"—to the supernatural. God has given man spirit from the beginning, and because of this the Holy Spirit is able to fashion marriage after something truly supernatural to it, the Head and Body, to which reality the image can constantly aspire.

Because of the nature of Christian marriage, the first effect of the sacrament, even before the giving of grace, is the union of husband and wife, or what is called the marriage bond. Fr. Palmer wrote:

> The bond is also an entity in the physical order, a kind of character uniting husband and wife in a special relationship with the mystical body of Christ, in which and through which the sacramental grace of marriage is received.... The bond is the first effect of marriage, antecedent by nature to grace and yet disposing husband and wife for the reception of grace if no obstacle is put in the way.[12]

The bond is not a sacramental character but is like it in that grace is given because of it. It is the union of two persons "in one flesh," in the whole biblical context of that phrase.

The role of the Holy Spirit in the Trinity is union of Father and Son; his role in the Mystical Body, consequently, is union—of members with the head, of members with each other, and of the whole with the Father. Therefore he is the first grace of matrimony—union for union. And, if husband and wife will yield their wills, led by the Spirit they will produce sons for God. To maintain marriage on this supernatural level grace is clearly necessary. The sanctifying grace of the sacrament provides the foundation for it. Pius XI had this to say of the sacra-

mental grace: "Hence this sacrament…also adds particular gifts, dispositions, seeds of grace, by elevating and
perfecting the natural powers."[13] He made a distinction
here: "Special gifts and germs of grace, which are an
amplification and perfection of the powers of nature,
enlightening the mind and strengthening the will;
and…the right to actual graces when they are needed."[14]
To see marriage first as the image of Christ and his
Church and always to act accordingly demands a super-
naturally enlightened intellect and a superhuman power
of will, which do come about by the special actual graces
given by the sacrament. On this point the Holy Father
warned:

> Nevertheless, since it is a law of divine
> Providence in the supernatural order that
> men do not reap the full fruit of the sacra-
> ments which they receive after acquiring the
> use of reason unless they cooperate with
> grace, the grace of matrimony will remain for
> the most part an unused talent hidden in the
> field unless the parties exercise these super-
> natural powers and cultivate and develop the
> seeds of grace they have received.[15]

Husband and wife minister this sacrament to each other
because the sacramental sign is the expression of their
mutual consent. Thus it is an action in which each gives
himself to the other (the matter), which giving receives
the meaning of fulfillment in acceptance (the form). With
regard to this mutual giving and acceptance as the symbolic action of the sacrament, Fr. Palmer's words about

the sacramental grace are apt: "Sharing through baptism in the priesthood of Christ, and acting as Christ's ministers of the sacrament, they give grace to each other. Their first and best wedding gift is the gift of grace."[16] This will have immeasurably more value if it follows upon a courtship in which each gave of self to the preservation of the life of grace in the other.

The setting of the sacrament of matrimony is the Eucharist. It is given during the Mass, as is also the nuptial blessing, and there are pertinent texts for the proper parts. However, from the biblical texts cited, we see a deeper relationship between matrimony and Eucharist. First of all, the term "Lamb," used for Christ in the book of Revelation, marks him as the Eucharistic victim, the paschal victim of the new covenant. Then the words of St. Paul in Ephesians, "devoid of blemish," applied to the Church as Bride of Christ, recalls this expression used many times in the Old Testament with regard to not only the paschal lamb but also sacrificial victims.[17] The Church unites herself to Christ as victim, for she as his Body is really one with him. In the Mass he offers both himself as the essential victim and his Church as his extended self. He has previously cleansed her "in the bath of water," as purification of the victim for sacrifice.[18] So husband and wife as image of the union of Christ and his Church find another exemplar in the Mass, an exemplar for their activity, one that will demand much meditation and that will determine their own offering of the Mass. Each will unite himself with Christ the victim, for the glory of the Father, for the needs of the Church, and only then for their own needs. By the Mass they will come to realize that Christian marriage transcends one that centers on itself. It aspires to the life of the Trinity.

Christian marriage is an epitome of most of the sacraments. The oneness of the wife with her husband derives from the fact that she is the image of the Church, who comes from the side of Christ by baptism. Husband and wife use their share in Christ's priesthood that the baptismal character gives when they give the sacrament to each other. Their concern for the Church, for building the Mystical Body, derives from the character and grace of confirmation. And lastly, they work with the priests of the Church in this process. This is, therefore, a sacrament that is most intimately bound to the life of the Church; it forms the very image of that life. Instead of being something profane that rises up from earth because of a ritual sanctification, it is rather something "...coming down out of heaven from God, surrounded with the divine glory."

Notes

1.   Eph 5:22-33. The quotation is from Genesis 2:24.
2.   Rv 21:9-10.
3.   Rom 5:14.
4.   Tertullian, *De Anima*, 43, in Jean Daniélou, S.J., *From Shadows to Reality* (Westminster, Md.: The Newman Press, 1960), p. 49.
5.   Jn 19:34.
6.   Daniélou, *op. cit.*, pp. 52-53.
7.   Gen 2:24; cf. Mt 19:4-6.

8.   Cf. Taymans d'Eypernon, S.J., *The Blessed Trinity and the Sacraments* (Westminster, Md.: The Newman Press, 1961), pp. 87-89.

9.   *The Missal* (Westminster, Md.: The Newman Press, 1958); Nicolas Zernov, *Eastern Christendom* (New York: G. P. Putnam's Sons, 1961), p. 254.

10.   Jn 17:21.

11.   Rom 5:5.

12.   Paul F. Palmer, S.J., *Sacraments of Healing and of Vocation* (Englewood Cliffs, N.J.: Prentice-Hall, 1963), pp. 97-98.

13.   Pius XI, *Casti Connubii, in Seven Great Encyclicals* (Glen Rock, N.J.: Paulist Press, 1963), p. 88.

14.   In Bernard Leeming, SJ, *Principles of Sacramental Theology* (Westminster: The Newman Press, 1962), p. 108.

15.   Pius XI, *op. cit.,* p. 89.

16.   Palmer, *op. cit.,* pp. 100-101.

17.   Cf. Ex 12:5; Lev 1:3, 10; 3:1, 6; Num 6:14.

18.   Cerfaux, *Christ in the Theology of St. Paul* (New York: Herder and Herder, 1960), p. 310.

INDEX